Iosco-Arenac Regional Library

Headquarters
Tawas City, Michigan

The

First Steamboat

on the Mississippi

NORTH STAR BOOKS

The
First Steamboat
on the Mississippi

STERLING NORTH

Illustrated by Victor Mays

1 9 6 2

HOUGHTON MIFFLIN COMPANY BOSTON

The Riverside Press Cambridge

Books by

STERLING NORTH

Plowing on Sunday
Night Outlasts the Whippoorwill
Seven Against the Years
The Pedro Gorino (with Captain Harry Dean)
Speak of the Devil (with Clip Boutell)
So Dear to My Heart
Reunion on the Wabash
The Birthday of Little Jesus
Abe Lincoln, Log Cabin to White House
Son of the Lampmaker
George Washington
Young Thomas Edison
Thoreau of Walden Pond
Captured by the Mohawks
Mark Twain and the River
The First Steamboat on the Mississippi

Contents

A Note on Sources

Writing a book about an almost forgotten man like Nicholas Roosevelt is a great adventure and a challenge. It takes sharp detective work, much digging through old letters and newspaper files, trips to many museums and libraries, and navigation on the waters Roosevelt knew so well.

The upper Ohio and the Mississippi have been known to me for many years. The Hudson has become almost as familiar in the last two decades. These mighty streams flow through the book in your hand.

It would be a long discourse were I to thank everyone who helped me find material on Nick and Lydia Roosevelt. Staff members of the Kingston Museum, the Roosevelt Library at Hyde Park, the New York Public Library and the Maryland Historical Society were particularly kind and cooperative. Scores of books and manuscripts have been consulted, among the most useful being: Chancellor Robert R. Livingston *by George Dangerfield;* Benjamin Henry Latrobe *by Talbot Hamlin;* Master of the Mississippi *by Florence L. Dorsey;* Steamboating on the Upper Mississippi *by William J. Petersen;* History of Steam Navigation *by John H. Morrison; the State Guide Series, and particularly that delightful little pamphlet,* The First Steamboat Voyage on the Western Waters *by J. H. B. Latrobe.*

But no book becomes completely real and alive without small pilgrimages to the scenes of action. We hope that all readers, young or old, will visit the Ohio and the Mississippi by car or by boat. The entire North Star series, in fact, is an invitation to see America, in depth — our beautiful and endangered land of fields and forests, mountains and rivers, cities and farms, worthy of every defense we can offer with pen or sword.

STERLING NORTH

For Gladys —

who understands why Lydia and Nick stood
side-by-side as the *New Orleans* plunged
through the Falls of the Ohio.

With similar devotion —

Sterling North

1

A Boy and His Boat

LIKE most boys, Nick Roosevelt liked to go fishing.
The opportunities were almost limitless, and so
were the fish in all the waters surrounding the little
City of New York in that still peaceful spring of
1775.

Starting at the Battery at the lower tip of Manhattan, docks and slips and sea walls ran for about
a mile up the East River, and also up the Hudson.
From any of these a fisherman might catch shad,
striped bass, and even salmon during their upstream
migration in the spring. Many varieties of fish from
tomcod to mighty sturgeon were to be found in
both rivers.

Young Nick Roosevelt, who was nearly eight

years old and big for his age, haunted the water-front, often with fishpole in hand. Fishhooks cost him not a penny, because his father owned a prosperous hardware store. Worms were to be had for the digging in the flourishing garden and orchard of his own home on Greenwich Street, not far from the Bowling Green at the foot of Broadway.

The wide plot surrounding the comfortable home of Jacobus, the hardware merchant, ran right down to the Hudson itself. Often young Nick, munching an apple or a peach from the heavily laden fruit trees, sat on the stone wall at the water's edge, idly fishing as he viewed with never-ending fascination the sailing ships from all over the world that came into this busy harbor. Sometimes, when the wind was from the north, a square-rigger might struggle for hours, beating its way up the harbor to safe anchorage. One of Nick's earliest thoughts — for he was a very thoughtful boy — centered around this problem. Wasn't there some better way to propel a ship? It would be many years before he discovered the answer.

Fishing from his own sea wall was a pleasant pastime, but very early in life young Nick showed desire for a dash of adventure. More imaginative than most of the early Roosevelts,* Nick had a sharply inquiring mind and scarcely any balance wheel of caution. Perhaps his own mother, had she lived, would have kept him from wandering so far afield. But his young stepmother Helena let Nick do very much as he pleased, particularly since the birth of her first baby, Ann, less than three months previously.

So, on this April morning, Nick slipped from his bed just before dawn, and taking his fishrod and worms, started northward on Broadway. Salt-water angling from the shore was tame sport when compared to luring the big trout that lurked in rushing Minetta Brook north of town.

It was a morning of swirling mists, rose-tinted in the East. The tower of Trinity Church disappeared, as though by magic, into the unknown upper air. The cobblestones of Broadway, washed by a night of showers, gleamed with moisture, and the great

---

* Claes Martenszen was the first Roosevelt to come to America, arriving in 1649. He was the great-great-great-great-great-grandfather of both Theodore Roosevelt and Franklin D. Roosevelt. The hero of our book, Nicholas Roosevelt, was in the fifth generation of the branch of the family which produced Theodore.

houses of wealthy neighbors swam into view and out again like castles under the sea.

Leaving the little city behind him, Nick skirted salt marshes where thousands of migrating water-fowl were pausing on their trip northward to their nesting grounds in the arctic. Canada geese, wild swans, mallards, canvasback, and teal started up with a whir of wings, fairly dancing along the surface of the water as they became air-borne, their cries muted by the fog. Collect Pond stretched beyond view, its near surface mirroring the mist. On higher land the fields and woods were sweet with rain, and with the scent of pine needles and of last year's leather-brown oak leaves.

Nick came at last to the rushing Minetta, winding along the edge of sandhills, leaping over ledges of rock and into likely pools. In a few minutes, now, he would be baiting his hook and tossing his line into the water where the larger trout always lay.

But at a curve in the brook a strange vision appeared. Nick knew that in reality this was a long, low, stone mill building and that the big, mossy wheel, slowly turning, was the waterwheel that

powered the machinery within. However, in the mist that drifted up the valley of the Minetta, all of the foreground and background were obscured.

The low-lying building appeared to be lost and alone on a vast and foggy sea, some strange sort of vessel propelled by the great wheel amidships. Nick almost held his breath as this floating apparition, without sails or oars, seemed to move with ghostly assurance through the ascending vapor.

A moment later the sun broke through and the illusion vanished. It was the old mill after all and no magic about it. Just below that mill lay one of the best trout holes in the entire stream.

Nick laughed, baited his hook, and with that pleasant sense of half-fearful anticipation that all fishermen have known, hopefully tossed his line into the dark, deep pool where lay the loveliest of all game fish — swift, wily and bold.

When Nick returned that afternoon with a fine string of trout, the town was ablaze with excitement. All twenty-five thousand of the citizens seemed to be talking, arguing, shouting or singing. An exhausted messenger had arrived from Boston with the news that the Minute Men of Lexington and Concord had fought a running battle with a column of redcoats sent to confiscate the secret caches of gunpowder collected by the patriots. Did this mean war against the mother country? Had the colonies reached the limit of their endurance? Would there be fighting here in New York as well as in Boston? Nick Roosevelt thought sadly that no one in the family seemed even slightly aware of his handsome catch of trout.

The Revolution came tardily to New York City.

The most strategic port in the New World continued to function uneasily as a British colonial town for nearly a year after the first skirmishes in Massachusetts.

For a time British officers in their scarlet coats and gold lace continued to promenade from the fort northward on Broadway, and in Trinity churchyard, escorting fashionable young women of the city, followed by their Negro servant girls at a discreet distance.

Some of the richer residents were outspokenly loyal to King George III. Others, equally wealthy, so resented that "long train of abuses" heaped upon the thirteen colonies that they were quietly sympathetic with the rowdy Sons of Liberty who erected liberty poles in defiance of the king.

The Roosevelts, who for a century and a quarter had been farmers, fur traders, tanners, millers, sugar refiners, goldsmiths, aldermen, shipowners, real estate speculators, and merchants of every variety, had much to lose and little to gain from open warfare on the Island of Manhattan.

Nevertheless, with but few exceptions they were patriots, many of them sacrificing money, property and even their lives for a cause much greater than self-interest.

For the moment, Jacobus, the hardware merchant, continued to sell his pots and pans, hammers and nails, crockery and other merchandise (meanwhile keeping his own counsel). Presumably there was little political talk in the household of this quiet patriot. Like his youngest son Nick, he was fundamentally more interested in things mechanical than things political.

While Nick roamed New York City investigating the entrancing machinery of windmills, horse mills and water mills, looking into the vats where leather was being tanned, tasting the sugar and molasses in the sugar refineries, and watching with utter fascination the gunsmiths fashioning death-dealing muskets, Boston to the northeast was fully at war. The battle of Bunker Hill was being fought, and the British Army was bottled up in Boston by colonial troops led by George Washington.

Actually two great revolutions were occurring simultaneously — the American Revolution and the

Industrial Revolution, and both were interrelated. It was principally England's attempt to smother colonial manufacture and trade that made the political revolt a necessity. King George and most of his ministers did not realize that no mother country can long suppress in her colonies such men as the Roosevelts. They will manufacture, transport and sell needful commodities despite all the stamp acts, navigation acts and other restrictive laws.

The City of New York that year was neither at war nor at peace, neither completely loyal nor completely disloyal to the Crown. Feeling began to run high against the British troops, and the royal governor, who soon withdrew to warships in the harbor. But the break was not yet complete, and the colony continued for some time to provision those menacing ships of the king's navy.

Not until March 1776 — a few days before the British were driven from Boston — did New Yorkers realize with great certainty that they too would soon hear gunfire. Washington had sent additional regiments to reinforce the small army on the Island of Manhattan, troops which were welcomed by cheering crowds. Fortified gun emplacements began to appear at the ends of streets running down to the Hudson and the East River. Cartloads of sod rumbled over the cobblestones on their way to the fort, to bolster its walls against naval bombardment.

Then two great events jolted the city from the last of its lethargy. One was the signing of the Declaration of Independence. The other was the gathering of such an invasion fleet as the New World had never previously seen. Four hundred and twenty-seven transports and fifty-two warships, manned by more than 10,000 British sailors and marines, moved into adjacent waters. At night thousands of British campfires could be seen flickering from the dark shores of Staten Island. On any warm evening when the Roosevelts stepped into their garden, or walked down to their sea wall, they could watch those ominous fireflies mirrored on the troubled surface of the great harbor.

And then, on a never-to-be-forgotten day in July, a copy of the Declaration of Independence arrived and was read to Washington and his troops drawn up on the Commons north of the city. Nick Roosevelt was there, and so were most of the rest of the citizens:

> We hold these truths to be self-evident, — that all men are created equal; that they are endowed by their Creator with certain inalienable rights; that among these are life, liberty and the pursuit of happiness . . .

Some of the listeners wept. Others glared fiercely toward the English sails in the harbor. And when the final words rang out, mutually pledging ". . . our lives, our fortunes and our sacred honor . . ." a cry that deepened into a roar burst from thousands of throats. As though driven by one mind and one will, a mob as wild as any America had ever seen rushed pell-mell toward the Bowling Green where with ropes and iron bars they pulled down the great gilded equestrian statue of George III. It furnished 4000 pounds of lead, soon to be melted into bullets to repel the king's own soldiers.

Jacobus realized that his family was no longer safe in New York City. His older son and daughters had long since left the family home. His principal

concern at the moment was for his wife Helena, her baby Ann, and Nick. These three he would send by sloop seventy-five miles up the Hudson to Kingston (Esopus) where he had arranged for their care at the home of his friend Joseph Oosterhaudt, a successful farmer living four miles from that village.

As for Jacobus himself, although he was fifty-one years of age, he must close his house and store as quickly as possible and join his militia regiment; for he too had pledged his life, his fortune and his sacred honor.

As the small sloop, crowded with refugees, moved under fitful breezes up the lordly Hudson, past miles of the Palisades on the New Jersey shore, then into the very heart of the eastern mountains, Nick and his young stepmother, holding baby Ann in her arms, watched the forested hills slipping away behind them.

Now they were deep in country settled by the Dutch. The little towns of low stone houses seemed ancient and ageless and forever peaceful. Now and then a larger house, with proud weathercock, and scrubbed stone steps, boasted a gable-end of gleaming Holland brick. In moments of calm the sloop scarcely moved — reflecting its image on the glassy water.

A sudden thunderstorm reverberating through this gorge reminded Helena to tell her stepson Nick that these were the ghosts of Henry Hudson's crew playing at bowls in the mountains. And who could deny that the strange lights flickering from mast top and bowsprit were the mischievous spirits who soured the milk whenever there was a storm? The Hudson then and now is magic country, haunted by the phantom of Captain Kidd and many another pirate; by ghostly music and the voices of Dutch sailors long since drowned or pierced by Indian arrows.

No spot along the Hudson was more steeped in old Dutch ways and superstitions than Kingston, halfway up the river to Albany, or the low, rambling stone farmhouse of Joseph Oosterhaudt and his plump, hard-working and kindly wife, where Nick was to spend the next seven years of his boyhood.

Although the Revolution took a sharp turn for

the worse during the last half of 1776, and although Washington was forced from Manhattan, and with a dwindling army was driven across New Jersey to the Delaware, Jacobus Roosevelt continued to be confident that his wife and two youngest children would be safe in Kingston. How great must have been his anxiety when he learned in the summer of 1777 that Kingston itself might be attacked.

The British strategy was to cut the colonies into two manageable halves. General "Gentleman Johnny" Burgoyne, driving south down Lake Champlain with a formidable army of redcoats, hoped to meet a British fleet forcing its way up the Hudson. We now know that the two enemy forces never did join, and that Burgoyne was decisively defeated at Saratoga. But this was scant comfort to Kingston where breathless couriers revealed that a strong British squadron was sailing up the Hudson.

Nick Roosevelt saw the brief "battle" of Kingston, viewing with awe the fleet of frigates and flatboats and the *bateaux* heavily manned by enemy troops, their bayonets gleaming and their crimson coats blazing in the sun.

The British considered Kingston, seat of the

New York State Senate, "a nursery for almost every villain in the country." It was a town that must be destroyed. So they silenced the small American shore battery and swarmed into this village of some two hundred homes and "reduced the place to ashes . . . not leaving a house" — with the single exception of the tavern where the British officers had been doing their carousing.

The Oosterhaudt farmhouse, four miles from town, was not endangered, nor were its occupants. Helena, little Ann, and adventuresome Nick were as safe as Jacobus had hoped they would be. But

the sight of that burning town and the wildly fleeing villagers was to remain engraved on Nick's
mind forever. The mere fact that the village was
soon rebuilt on the original stone walls and foun-
dations did not lessen the bitterness every King-
stonian would feel for decades toward the ruthless
redcoats.

Nick was growing in mind and in body. His
restless imagination and his joy in the use of tools
marked him as an inventor while still in his early
teens. During the late summer of the year 1781
this sturdy thirteen-year-old boy awoke one morning with the excited realization that this was the
day he had been working and planning for.

It was not yet dawn, and the light was still dim
in the low-ceilinged farmhouse of Joseph Oosterhaudt, when Nick slipped quietly from his bed,
tiptoed down the steep stairway, and helped himself to a pewter jug of milk.

The kitchen had a Dutch half door (to keep
chickens out and children in). For a few moments
while he drank his milk, Nick gazed out through
the opened upper half of that wide door toward

the blue hills, just awakening in the predawn light. Then he hurried to the workbench in the barn where, with the good farmer's tools, he had fashioned a little wooden boat which would one day become the model for most of the river craft in the entire United States.

Years later in an affidavit defending his invention Nicholas testified that in this year he did

> . . . make, rig and put in operation, on a small brook near the house of the aforesaid Oosterhaudt, a small wooden boat or model of a boat with vertical wheels over the sides, each wheel having four arms or paddles, or floats made of pieces of shingle attached to the periphery of the wheels whereby to take a purchase on the water; and that these wheels being acted upon by . . . whalebone springs propelled the model of the boat through the water by the agency of a tight cord . . .

Clutching his model, Nick hurried down the path to the brook. The cool dew was pleasant to his bare and callused feet. At the pool where he so often fished and swam he drew a long breath, bent the whalebone spring and wound the cord tightly around the axle which was fastened securely to the paddle wheels.

Just as the sun was beginning to show its glowing rim over the hills on the far side of the Hudson, he prepared to launch his boat upon the stream. Still fearful that, for all his hard work, the boat might fail, he released his little vessel for its maiden voyage.

Swift as any fish or waterbird it darted away, braving the current of the brook. The bent whalebone slowly straightened, the cord unwound driving the little paddle wheels so fast that Nick could scarcely see the individual paddles. Spray from the wheels glistened in the light of the rising sun.

For the sun had now really arisen upon a new day. The first side-wheeler in the world had just been launched. And a thirteen-year-old boy was overwhelmingly aware that the future was bright with hope and promise.

2

Nick and His Nation Come of Age

ONE OTHER great and hopeful event marked this memorable year in Nick's life — a joy which he shared with every patriot in the thirteen colonies. General Cornwallis and his entire army were so decisively defeated at Yorktown, Virginia, that even the stubborn British now knew they had lost the war.

However, peace negotiations dragged on interminably, and enemy troops continued to occupy New York City for two additional years.

When a provisional treaty was approved in the spring of 1783, several thousand terrified Loyalists, who had sympathized with the British throughout the war, fled from New York. And although the redcoats remained in possession of the town until November, many erstwhile residents began to return to their homes — or the charred ruins where their homes had stood.

An excitement verging on hysteria gripped the Hudson River Valley. Refugees exiled from the city for seven long years were frantic to return to their beloved town to see what had happened to their property, and to begin life where it had been so rudely broken off in 1776. A letter of that period vividly reveals the mood then prevailing:

"The sloops go down, and such numbers of people flock to them that they are fighting for their passage — farmers are selling their farms to go and settle in Town; in short to go down is all the rage."

Sometime during the late summer or early autumn of 1783 Jacobus came to Kingston to take his wife Helena, little Ann, and fifteen-year-old Nick back to New York. Nick's father, now in his late fifties, had survived seven years of hardship while fighting the British. But the lines marking his weather-beaten face were not from war-weariness alone but also from worry about the future. Would they find their once-comfortable home on Greenwich Street burned or wrecked? Would the store across the street be in ashes?

As the sloop came booming down the Hudson ahead of a brisk wind, their first view of New York was anything but reassuring. The spire of Trinity was a black ruin. Broadway was burned out on both sides of the street for almost its entire length. What had once been a pleasant town of shaded streets, orchards, and gardens was now in some areas almost as desolate as a battlefield, owing to the havoc caused by two great fires and lesser depredations during British occupancy. Fuel had been so scarce that almost every tree had been cut down and many empty houses had been wrecked to be burned board by board. The Roosevelts, seeing all this from the deck of the sloop, felt their hearts sink with fear and desperation.

But as the little sailing boat came nearer to the Battery, Nick uttered a whoop of joy. There, safe and sound, stood their handsome waterside home, to all outward appearances in excellent shape. Their orchard had been cut down, but Jacobus already was making plans to plant a new one. And

then came another miraculous revelation! Yes, it was astonishingly true, the store across the street was still standing. Doubtless it had been stripped of its merchandise, but at least the building remained.

These Roosevelts, like some of the Livingstons and other well-to-do families, were among the lucky ones. Many of the finest houses had been occupied by important British officers, who maintained them well, and in some instances even added a room or two or a piazza in the garden.

Now their hearts could beat again.

All of the city turned out on the bright November day when the last of the British troops embarked. A New York woman who witnessed this historic event wrote of the scarlet uniforms and burnished arms of the British in contrast to the "ill-clad and weatherbeaten troops," marching in good order behind George Washington on his proud gray horse. "But then they were *our* troops, and as I thought upon all they had done and suffered for us, my heart and my eyes were full, and I admired and gloried in them the more, because they *were* weatherbeaten and forlorn."

Through crowds that cheered and wept for joy, the column moved southward toward the Fort. Fortunately a company of Light Infantry and one of Artillery had been sent ahead to raise the Stars and Stripes on the tall flagpole where for seven years the British flag had floated with such arrogant assurance. But the pole, though left standing, had been greased by the redcoats as a final insult. Soldier after soldier tried to climb that pole, with humiliating if hilarious results. Finally a sailor solved the problem by nailing cleat above cleat to the top of the pole. And there he fastened "the most beautiful flag in the world" — the new American flag with its thirteen stars and thirteen stripes.

By the time Washington and his column reached the scene, the national emblem was floating bravely in the breeze, while the artillery roared its thirteen-gun salute.

Had Jacobus Roosevelt been reduced to poverty, young Nick almost certainly would have put his strong shoulder to the wheel to help his father regain security. But Jacobus owned his house, and his store, and had the credit (if not the dollars) to quickly reopen his business.

In fact the whole city soon showed promise of an almost miraculous recovery. Despite the vast physical devastation, ruinous inflation, and all the other miseries which so often follow a war, the residents began to rebuild, repair, and replant with a spirit of faith and hope rare in any era.

Every sort of commodity was soon in great demand. As new houses and stores and other buildings rose from the ashes, Jacobus was besieged with demands for hinges and locks, hammers and saws, fire irons and weathercocks — in fact everything conceivable in the way of hardware needed by the town in its task of reconstruction. Business was so good that Nick's brother, James J. Roosevelt,* started another hardware store of his own in Maiden Lane, and this also soon was thriving.

Nick would have been welcome at either establishment. But he knew that he was not cut out to be a merchant. He was a dreamer, a schemer, and

---

* James J. Roosevelt was the great-grandfather of President Theodore Roosevelt.

an artisan in a new world suddenly free of the hampering British restrictions against manufacture. What he most needed was mechanical knowledge, greater skill in the handling of tools, and the ability to draw on paper the plans for the various machines he was continually inventing or adapting.

Nicholas Roosevelt — throughout life — was spoken of as an educated man. Possibly some kindly dominie in Kingston had tutored him. Perhaps he received a few years of formal schooling when he came back to New York. But it is highly unlikely that he attended the College (once known as King's, now Columbia). Here the entrance requirements demanded "a rational account of the Latin and Greek grammars, a reading of the first three of Tully's *Select Orations* and the first three books of the *Aeneid*, and a translation of the first ten chapters of St. John's Gospel from Greek into Latin."

Robert R. Livingston and John Jay had passed these "simple" requirements with flying colors and had gone on to become brilliant statesmen. But Nick Roosevelt's mind ran in another channel. He was articulate and stubbornly logical, but he had less interest in the classics than in the shaping of metal, the gearing of machinery, and the application of the power of steam to everything movable. In all this he was years ahead of most of his American contemporaries.

Nick may have been apprenticed briefly to some "master mechanic." It is more likely that he did a great deal of tinkering on his own where his vivid imagination and sensible deductions would not have been hampered by a hidebound employer.

Never during these years did he forget his model boat, and very early he began dreaming of powering those paddle wheels with steam. His excitement was intense when he learned that a brilliant but eccentric clockmaker and silversmith named John Fitch had constructed, on the Delaware River, a boat run by steam, propelling several oars "like canoe paddles" on each side of the boat — a considerable craft capable of carrying both freight and passengers.

But Nick still shook his head in doubt. Mechanically operated paddles would surely be clumsy, inefficient, and even dangerous to the passengers. The right way to send a boat through the water was by means of his own invention — "wheels over the sides." He wished he might build such a boat, but first he must work diligently and save all the money he could to help finance such a project. None of his hardheaded relatives would put a Continental dollar into such a feather-brained contraption.

Between 1783 and 1788 while Nick was growing from a fifteen-year-old boy to a young man of twenty, he acquired so much technical skill that he was considered one of the finest "mechanics" in the city. Nick and his country were growing up together, and in a most congenial way, since the very progress of the nation was based upon an economic foundation of manufacture and transportation.

New York was exuberantly optimistic, particularly after news arrived on July 2, 1788, that the tenth state had ratified the new Constitution, thus putting the document into immediate effect. A tremendous Constitution Parade was planned — a demonstration which proved again how closely industry and political freedom were allied.

Nick probably participated in this gala event since "mechanics" of all sorts were its chief instigators.

The procession started "in the fields" (City Hall

Park) and wound by devious ways through the entire town with such an array of becostumed paraders, decorated floats, military escorts in dress uniform, horsemen with trumpets, stuffed bears, Indian chiefs in full regalia, and displays by butchers, bakers, and candlestick makers that the entire crowd was drunk with happiness even before they began drinking the thirteen toasts, each punctuated by the thunder of ten field pieces.

The bakers carried a loaf of bread ten feet long and three feet wide inscribed with the names of the thirteen states. The brewers had a great wagon loaded with barrels, festooned with hopvines, and topped by a throne in which sat a youthful Bacchus in flesh-colored silk, holding a huge silver goblet in his hand.

Ten milk-white horses pulled the 27-foot model of a thirty-two gun frigate, *Hamilton*. This "ship-of-state" so excited the captain of a real Spanish warship in the harbor that he honored the float with a thirteen-gun salute.

On came the painters, bricklayers, stone masons, cabinetmakers, upholsterers, furriers, tanners, wigmakers, coopers and apprentices and journeymen of these and a score of other crafts and trades. Then came printers, bookbinders, stationers, lawyers, physicians, university professors, and members of Congress. A banquet for six thousand was served in a beautiful pavilion provided for the purpose.

Nick Roosevelt realized as never before what an enormous contribution industry and the crafts were making toward the progress of the new republic so recently conceived in liberty.

A less flamboyant but more deeply moving celebration stirred the city on the following April when George Washington, the newly elected first President of the United States, arrived from Mount Vernon for the presidential inauguration.

As his flower-decorated barge landed at the foot of Wall Street, every church bell in New York was ringing its greeting.

Special steps had been constructed, and carpets laid, making his ascension to the wharf a matter of some elegance. But instead of taking the "chariot" awaiting him, he walked through the crowded streets, "attended by Governor Clinton, army officers and gentlemen."

Just as the sun arose on April 30, 1789, the guns of the old fort boomed over the harbor. From nine to nine-thirty the bells of all the churches pealed, rather sedately, as congregations in every church prayed for "the blessings of Heaven" on the new President, and beseeched the Almighty for the protection of George Washington and his young nation.

At high noon a military escort assembled in Cherry Street before the house where the President was waiting. They were often the same men, but in appearance far different from the "weatherbeaten and forlorn" troops of less than six years ago. Now they wore dress uniforms, "in blue with red facings and gold-laced ornaments, cocked hats with white feathers, with waistcoats and breeches and white garters."

Nick Roosevelt viewed with curiosity, pride, and tenderness these gestures of affection and honor to the man who had suffered with his troops at Valley Forge and Morristown. He was among the dense crowd at the corner of Wall and Broad Streets — so thick "one might literally walk on the heads of people" — when George Washington accompanied by Vice-President elect John Adams, Governor Clinton and other notables stepped onto the balcony of stately Federal Hall. Then from several thousand viewers arose such a cheer as even their venerable leader had never previously heard.

Chancellor Robert Livingston read the Oath of Office, and the old soldier now chosen by his people to be our President repeated it slowly and thoughtfully before the multitude now "hushed in profound silence." The Stars and Stripes were raised on the cupola of the Hall to signal a general discharge of every piece of artillery at the Battery.

And once again the bells of the city rang out "a great peal of joy."

The United States had come of age. And so had 21-year-old Nicholas Roosevelt — from whose family would emerge one day two other great American Presidents who would also take this solemn Oath of Office.

3

Steamboat on the Passaic

AT WHAT is now called Belleville, New Jersey, not far up the Passaic River from Newark, a deep dark shaft went into the ground from the top of Schuyler Hill. This had once been a successful copper mine, but the workings had extended to such a great depth that the best copper ore was 360 feet below the riverbed. Quite understandably, water had filled the old mine shaft to the river level, and no pumps operated by horsepower had been efficient enough to drain this subterranean cavern.

General Philip Schuyler (for whom that hill was named) wanted to reopen his mine. This veteran of the French and Indian War and the American Revolution was an able and patriotic man, now sixty years of age. Like Chancellor Livingston he was the scion of a great landholding family of upper New York state. And in further similarity to Livingston, his political power and his vast estates always exceeded his ready cash.

General Schuyler heard of the mechanical ability of Nicholas Roosevelt, now in his mid-twenties, and offered him a partnership if he could drain and work the mine. Nick had the technical skill, and some of the needed money to accept the challenge. He also had an intimate knowledge of steam engines gained by carefully examining the few which had been imported from Boulton and Watt of Birmingham, England. In this field he equaled or surpassed any engineer then living in America. And he was tremendously excited by his new assignment, throwing himself into the venture with all his energy and imagination.

It is difficult to visualize a time when the United States, now the greatest industrial country in the world, had not a single foundry or machine shop capable of producing a simple steam engine. But such was the case in 1793 when Nick Roosevelt promised he would drain the Schuyler mine.

Both General Schuyler and his young partner agreed that it would be far better to construct steam engines and pumps on this side of the Atlantic if that were possible. So Nick set up a factory patterned upon the Boulton and Watt model in Birmingham. And in honor of that pilot plant across the Atlantic, he named this new machine shop "Soho." With about a dozen assistants, including two expert mechanics from the Boulton and Watt company, Roosevelt was soon constructing steam engines which were about as good as any he could have imported. With these he swiftly pumped the Schuyler copper mine dry.

Apparently the ore body below the 360-foot level was not rich enough to allow the mine to make money on its operation. But the engine works — the only one of its kind in the country — was soon on a sound and paying basis.

Now to the Soho machine shop came Chancellor Robert R. Livingston, a most distinguished visitor. This fourth-generation Scots-American landlord of the upper Hudson River was brilliant in law and politics, a progressive gentleman farmer, and an avid amateur in the realm of mechanics. Nick Roosevelt knew, of course, that the Chancellor had been one of the committee serving with Thomas Jefferson in framing the Declaration of Independence, and that he had written most of the New York State Constitution.

As Nick had seen with his own eyes, it was Livingston who had been granted the privilege and honor of administering the oath of office to President Washington.

When this silken diplomat and jurist arrived at the Soho works he may well have discovered Nick smeared with grease and metal dust and at work on one of his steam engines. Between Livingston's deafness and the noise of the machine shop, Nick doubtless thought it best to take the Chancellor to "Laurel Hill" — his beautiful home on a rise above the Passaic. Excusing himself long enough to bathe and dress, Nick could then talk to the Chancellor on more nearly equal terms, and satisfy his overwhelming curiosity as to the reason for this visit.

Livingston had apparently heard of Nick's talent

and perseverance from General Schuyler, and he had a proposition to make which sent young Roosevelt's head swimming.

Here was the chance for which Nick had been waiting, the opportunity to construct a steamboat in partnership with a gentleman who could finance the venture. As Roosevelt listened, his enthusiasm mounted. Nick was to be allowed to build the steam engine for a boat to be launched here at the Soho works.

But after a few hours of conversation Roosevelt's ardor cooled a trifle as he learned some of the other and less pleasing conditions. The boat itself was to be designed by Livingston's brother-in-law John Stevens, and the method of locomotion? — well, Livingston would be writing Nick on this matter! "Wheels over the sides," Roosevelt immediately suggested, "the only possible way to drive a steamship through the water."

Chancellor Livingston had one of his convenient deaf spells and didn't quite catch what Nick was saying. He really must get back to his estate, Clermont-on-the-Hudson, from which manorial

address he would be writing at length on all developments.

Despite many differences which soon arose between Livingston and Roosevelt, an agreement was signed during the month of April 1798, and work immediately commenced upon the hull of the boat and the engine. In that same month a patent was granted which has been overlooked by virtually every steamboat historian.

That Roosevelt showed brilliance in designing the power plant for this boat is amply proved by long-forgotten evidence which has just come to light in the archives of the Roosevelt Library at Hyde Park. This fascinating original document, in copper-plate script, is a patent signed by John Adams, Timothy Pickering, and Charles Lee.* It grants to Nicholas J. Roosevelt and James Smallman (one of the expert mechanics formerly employed by Boulton and Watt) a patent for "a double steam engine, which improvement has not been known or used before." This would seem to mean that Roosevelt and Smallman had hit upon the principle of the reciprocating steam engine, since the patent gives them full rights to a device consisting of "two air pumps . . . so constructed as to make the vacuum perfect both ways, which gives our engines of thirty inches cylinder five and five-sevenths Horses power more than the highly famed engines which are built by Messrs. Watt and Boulton."

Nicholas Roosevelt now had the two great principles which were to make river steamboats feasible — a good marine steam engine, and "wheels over

* Respectively President, Secretary of State, and Attorney General of the United States.

the sides." He was a thorough professional and knew precisely what he was doing.

But Livingston, always the amateur in mechanics and invention, not only resisted the engine design but absolutely vetoed "wheels over the sides."

Livingston came of stubborn Scots blood. Roosevelt came of stubborn Dutch blood. And the head-on collision of these two stubborn men came near to sinking the Passaic River steamboat before it was ever launched. Nick was right and the Chancellor was perversely wrong, but Livingston was supplying the money, and in the end Roosevelt was forced to make a compromise. If the steam engine could be built according to his own plans, he would let the Chancellor have his way concerning the means of locomotion.

Much of Livingston's correspondence was not made available to scholars until quite recently. But in exchanges with the Chancellor we find Nick insisting for several months upon "two wheels of wood over the sides, fashioned to the axes of the flys with 8 arms or paddles." Stevens meanwhile wanted elliptical paddle wheels, while the almost whimsical Livingston continued to insist upon a wheel on a vertical axis operating within a wooden box or flume fastened beneath the boat. In short, he dreamed of a primitive variety of jet propulsion, sending the boat forward by means of water expelled at the rear.

Nick knew it wouldn't work, and his two expert mechanics developed an intense dislike for the Chancellor and all of his weird ideas. But the boat was constructed with that flume beneath the keel; and the results were exactly those Roosevelt had predicted.

On a day in October 1798, Roosevelt, and a small company including the Spanish Minister, made a trial run on the Passaic. *Against* the wind and the tide the new steamboat progressed at approximately one mile an hour. *With* wind and tide, it went more swiftly, thrilling the Spanish Minister, who knew as little about mechanics as did that other statesman, Chancellor Livingston. Nick calculated that in still water his boat might average three miles an hour. Despite Livingston's plea that he bring it around to the Hudson for another test,

Roosevelt wisely refused. He knew the boat was a failure, and he wanted no more public demonstrations of its weaknesses.

Had Livingston been willing to listen to his young partner, and had the powerful new steam engine been allowed to spin "wheels over the sides," Nicholas Roosevelt would have anticipated Robert Fulton's "invention" by about nine years, and Roosevelt, not Fulton would have been remembered as the father of steam navigation.

4

Roosevelt Meets Latrobe and Lydia

ANOTHER year rolled around, and another interesting visitor arrived at Laurel Hill with yet another challenging proposal.

The new arrival was Benjamin Henry Latrobe, a strikingly handsome man, six feet two inches in height, with flashing dark eyes, quick wit, and more knowledge packed within his well-shaped head than was possessed by any man Roosevelt had ever encountered.

Latrobe, who came of aristocratic French Huguenot stock, had mastered eight languages including Greek, Latin, and Hebrew. Educated in England and in Germany, he had acquired an excellent

Latrobe

professional training under the engineer Smeaton
and the architect Cockerell.

Although he had been on this side of the Atlantic
for less than three years, he was already building
the most ambitious project in Philadelphia — the
new waterworks, which promised to channel the
clean water of the Schuylkill River to a city then
dependent upon polluted wells.

To accomplish his difficult engineering feat,
Latrobe needed two enormous steam engines, and
Nicholas Roosevelt was the only man in America
who could build them.

This amiable meeting, which was to mean so much in both of their lives, occurred in October 1799 during a tense political moment sometimes called the "Undeclared Naval War with France." The French Revolution, which at first was hailed by a great majority of our citizens, had turned into a very bloody and dictatorial affair. Our ships were being attacked by France on the high seas. President John Adams — although he wanted peace — was beefing up our navy as a defensive measure.

At least four new 74-gun frigates — probably as strong, ship-for-ship, as any vessels in the French fleet — were currently being constructed. And Nicholas Roosevelt had been awarded the important contract to buy and roll the sheet copper to sheath their hulls.

Roosevelt was deep in the risky business of purchasing many tons of raw copper and rolling it for the frigates.

Latrobe was involved in the equally risky business of digging a canal, installing engines, and designing the huge waterworks, underwriting an almost inexhaustible source of clean water for Philadelphia.

Both men — like so many daring pioneers — had

more imagination and talent than business sense.

They were of almost equal height, brilliance, charm — and impetuosity. They were mercurial, gentle, literate and sensitive. Our best assurance that Nicholas Roosevelt was a well-educated man comes from Latrobe himself (who almost certainly was the greater scholar). He spoke frequently throughout his life of Roosevelt's culture and complete integrity. Within a matter of days, during that late October, they became the most important and steadfast friends either would ever know. But they also enmeshed themselves in financial difficulties which would haunt them both for the next fifteen years.

To obtain the needed raw copper — far beyond any ore the Schuyler mine could produce — Nick had involved himself in debts which ran into many thousands of dollars. To build the engines and pumps for Philadelphia, both he and Latrobe would have to pledge personally owned real estate amounting to every acre of land the two men possessed. The Navy, and the City of Philadelphia, were taking no chances.

It would necessitate the services of a Philadelphia

lawyer (and several were subsequently involved) to determine what next transpired. Almost immediately Latrobe signed notes to help cover Roosevelt's copper purchases for the Navy; and Roosevelt signed notes to help cover Latrobe's waterworks investment in behalf of the City of Philadelphia.

They were already friends in the least selfish sense — willing to help each other to the limit of their resources or go down together.

Their conversation ranged happily over a dozen mutual interests — books, engineering, art, architecture, steamships, and what should be done to improve and complete the new and unfinished Capitol and President's House in Washington — assignments which Jefferson soon would be trusting to Latrobe. And of course Roosevelt agreed to build the steam engines.

On their final day of this visit they talked of more personal things. To describe the view from the terrace in terms of copper and its ores, the Passaic River was malachite, pale green, as it is even today. The sky was azurite, an intense blue. And the leaves of the trees were burnished copper itself.

It is probable that the architect at this time told Nicholas Roosevelt of his two bright children still in England, Lydia and Henry Latrobe, offspring by his first beloved wife, now dead. Nearly three years of separation from these children had multiplied the father's longing to see them — particularly beautiful little Lydia. And it is quite possible that Nick — sight unseen — fell in love with this growing girl on that October afternoon as Roosevelt and Latrobe looked off across the river toward the far horizon.

Benjamin Henry Latrobe, although emotional and optimistic, was no fool. He was a builder of canals and cathedrals, an artist, a prose stylist, a linguist and a man of the world. When he disliked and distrusted an associate or competitor he could express his distaste in stinging phrases. It is therefore of considerable importance that through many years of financial misery and discouragement in partnership with Nicholas Roosevelt he seldom allowed himself more than a kindly word or two of criticism.

To his brother Christian he wrote:

> Mr. Roosevelt is a man of exceptionally good moral character — and is of one of the oldest families of the State of New York — has a handsome fortune and inhabits one of the most enchanting seats in Jersey [Laurel Hill] on the river Passaic.

Latrobe's friend, Thomas Jefferson, came to the Presidency in 1801. Almost immediately he canceled the contract for the frigates and their copper sheathing. This came very near to bringing both Roosevelt and Latrobe to ruin. (For in those frugal days the United States government did not make financial settlement for canceled contracts.)

Similar disasters, surrounding the strikingly successful Philadelphia waterworks, brought both men even nearer to bankruptcy. In each instance these skilled technicians had triumphed on an engineering level while being defeated on the political level. There lay the shining useless copper, beautifully rolled for the Navy's frigates. There stood the handsome waterworks, delivering sparkling water to Philadelphia. But the Navy and the City Fathers of Philadelphia saw no reason for adequately compensating Roosevelt and Latrobe. The small cash recompence to these hard-working partners could scarcely have been more disasterous.

However, one of the dreams of that autumn visit continued to burgeon and bear fruit. This dream concerned Lydia, the spirited and handsome daughter of Latrobe.

Benjamin Henry Latrobe had hesitated to bring his daughter and son to America chiefly because, as a widower, his lonely existence furnished a poor substitute for the home environment his children needed. Now, however, this lack was to be remedied. The engineer-architect met and fell in love with Mary Elizabeth Hazlehurst, a warm, wise, loyal and socially adept young woman who filled a great void in his melancholy heart. They were married on May 2, 1800 — and one of the bride's first requests was that her husband send for his two children in England.

On their honeymoon trip to New York, Latrobe and his wife stopped for several days at Laurel Hill to see Nicholas Roosevelt, who from this moment on became "part of the family." In October the two children, in charge of a responsible adult, arrived from England and almost immediately were happily adjusted to their new mother and home in Philadelphia.

Visiting back and forth between Laurel Hill and Philadelphia was frequent and Nicholas played the part of a young "uncle" to Lydia, Henry, and the new crop of children which soon began to arrive. Nick watched with tender approval as Lydia grew from a sprightly ten-year-old into a thoughtful pre-adolescent, wise and mature beyond her years. In this household where music, art, literature, and languages were common table talk, the mental

stimulation to the children had all the good effects of sunshine and rain upon a garden of flowers.

Lydia proved to be an excellent aid to her stepmother in caring for little John, Juliana, Benjamin Henry, and the others as they came along. She was gentle but firm, and also playful, only occasionally showing a trace of high-spirited temper. This lovely girl was also an excellent nurse when any member of the family was ill, and from her thirteenth year proved capable of running the entire household in her parents' absence. A short term of formal schooling at fashionable Jaudon's Academy added a final touch of social ease.

Then the explosion of early adolescence transformed her in a few months from a child into a stunningly handsome young woman. Sometime late in 1804 — when Lydia was going on fourteen — "Uncle Nick" saw her as though through completely new eyes. And for the first and last time in his life he fell desperately in love.

When Roosevelt wrote to Mrs. Latrobe, frankly stating his love, the letter burst like a bomb in the architect's household. Latrobe, in one of his few critical letters to his closest associate, stated his utter amazement, and said that on this delicate subject it would be better to "*talk* than to *write*. Perhaps it will be still better to *laugh*." Lydia, he reminded Nick, was not yet fourteen, though "a fine sensible young woman, inheriting . . . her mother's character as to unevenness of temper, but abounding also in qualities of solid virtue."

In short, Latrobe was in a turmoil of conflicting emotions. His best friend wanted to marry his little daughter. He loved and admired them both, and wanted nothing but their happiness. However he rightly believed that Lydia was too young to marry, and there were other arguments against the union.

Roosevelt's finances were now as precarious as his own.

Like Latrobe himself, he was headstrong, overly optimistic and impulsive.

Finally there was the greatest obstacle of all, the differences in their ages — Nick being more than twenty years older than Lydia.

Mary Latrobe was not quite so disturbed as her husband. She pointed out the fact that Juliet was only fourteen when she secretly married Romeo. And she also added that gay, kindly flamboyant

Dolly Madison was more than twenty years younger than her famous husband, little James Madison — and that *that* marriage seemed to be a happy one.

But none of these arguments made much sense to Latrobe, who was driven to near distraction by Lydia, who became so disturbed over her father's objections that she was "seized with a dreadful affection — as affected as a cat."

Latrobe again wrote Roosevelt, disclosing Lydia's melancholy. "I don't know what to do with her," he admitted to the equally love-lorn Nicholas.

Latrobe forbade Lydia to write to Nick, but for several years they carried on a secret correspondence, filled with avowals of love, impetuous proposals, and despair.

It is true that Lydia was unable to completely avoid all the young naval officers who appeared at the Latrobe entertainments held in their new home in Washington. But she gave none of these suitors her heart or her hand. She was waiting, waiting quite desperately now, for Nicholas.

The years 1805, 1806, and 1807 passed unhappily for the lovers. But Latrobe could not hold the fortress indefinitely and in September 1808 he gave his approval. On November 15 of that year, in the Latrobe house in Washington, Lydia and Nicholas were married by "the Revd. Mr. McCormick." Only a few of their closest friends were present, but one of them was Dolly Madison, the living proof that "May can happily marry September."

Handsome Nicholas stood beside radiant Lydia to pledge their love "till death us do part" — an oath they faithfully kept throughout their lives. And so began years of high adventure.

5

By Flatboat to New Orleans

WHILE Nicholas Roosevelt had been deeply involved in his business problems and his troubled courtship of Lydia Latrobe, his ex-partner, Robert R. Livingston, had been making history in Paris.

President Thomas Jefferson had sent the Chancellor to France on an urgent and delicate mission — the proposal to buy from Napoleon the port city of New Orleans — gateway to the Mississippi River and the entire mid-American continent.

As the president expressed it in a letter to his envoy:

There is on the globe one single spot, the possessor of which is our natural and habitual enemy. It is New Orleans, through which the produce of three-eighths of our territory must pass to market, and from its fertility it will ere long yield more than half of our whole produce and contain more than half of our inhabitants.

Jefferson was not the only American who was firm in this belief. Recent difficulties with the New Orleans officials had set the entire region west of the Alleghenies ablaze with anger. Flatboats filled with corn and hogs, lumber, hemp, country linen, dried fruit and beans, flour, bacon and pork, and hundreds of barrels of whiskey and cider were tied up at many a creek and landing, waiting to float down to New Orleans, their only possible market. It was a matter of fight or starve for these frontiersmen, and they preferred to fight. Cabin dwellers took down their rifles from their hickory pegs. Carved powder horns were filled with fresh powder, and many bullets were molded. No Frenchman or Spaniard could intimidate these rugged Indian fighters.

Thomas Jefferson and Chancellor Livingston were just as determined as the buckskin-clad frontiersmen to secure the invaluable port. But their methods were not those of the frontier. With a keen understanding of international politics and the game of diplomacy they made plans to purchase New Orleans from Napoleon at a moment when they felt sure he could not refuse their offer.

The smooth and wily Chancellor was up against two of the most brilliant and unscrupulous men France has ever produced: Bonaparte, the "Corsican Bandit" soon to proclaim himself emperor, and his foreign minister, the cool, cynical, double-dealing and diabolically clever Talleyrand.

It is true that Livingston's mastery of the French language was not sufficiently acute to follow every nuance of the swift conversation. But he could always use his deafness conveniently, asking Talleyrand to repeat a word or two, or asking for a written version of any oral proposal.

The Chancellor had been empowered to offer three million dollars for the City of New Orleans and a small additional area. But both Napoleon and Talleyrand knew that the entire vast Louisiana Territory west of the Mississippi was all but worthless to them without the port. And Livingston did

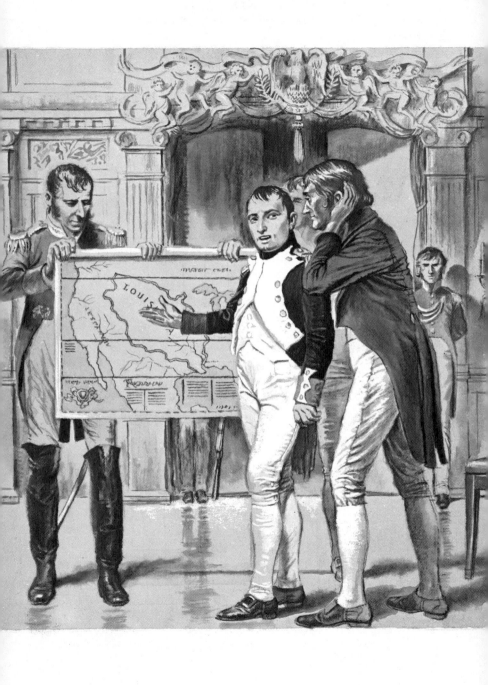

not hesitate to insinuate that during the next out-
break of war between France and England, the
British would seize the prize if American frontiersmen had not already taken it.

Livingston was pleased but not completely
amazed when Napoleon offered to sell not only the
city, but the whole of Louisiana Territory to the
United States at an unheard-of bargain — fifteen
million dollars. Here was an area five times the size
of continental France — an empire larger than
Napoleon could ever hope to conquer, being virtually given away for a few cents an acre. Here
were mountains, rivers, fertile plains, forests and
mineral wealth beyond the dream of any monarch
— one million square miles *plus* the city of New
Orleans. Livingston could not delay his decision
long enough for letters to cross the Atlantic — so
he boldly accepted the offer, and with James Monroe
closed the deal. Not a drop of blood had been
spilled in doubling the area of our new and expand-
ing nation. If Chancellor Livingston had done
nothing else for his country, he would still be
worthy of the eternal gratitude of every American,
then and since.

Robert Livingston was not wholly selfless, however. In addition to his admirable patriotism and public service, he was an aristocratic landowner and jurist who believed it his natural right to enjoy any monopoly he could grasp. Since the days when he and Nicholas Roosevelt had collaborated on the unsuccessful steamboat, he had been securing from the state of New York repeated renewals of a monopoly allowing him to own and operate the only steamboats to be permitted on the Hudson River and other waters of the state.

There was but one flaw in this private concession. To hold his monopoly he had to build and operate a successful steamboat.

In Paris, Livingston met the talented young painter and inventor Robert Fulton with whose name and fame he has ever since been connected. Fulton began his useful and creative life as a Pennsylvania jeweler. He had come to Europe to study painting under his compatriot Benjamin West, and had made many influential friends in England and France. Charming, handsome and quick-witted, Fulton impressed Livingston with his art, his inventions, and his lively conversation.

Livingston, still fighting for his monopoly, and therefore needful of producing a practical steamboat, told Fulton of his experiences with Nicholas Roosevelt (not hesitating to reveal Nick's insistent belief in "wheels over the sides"). In his new partnership with Fulton, Livingston financed the construction of two model steamboats which were tested on the river Seine not far from Paris. The second and more successful of these models was equipped with the paddle wheels which Roosevelt had long suggested.

When Livingston and Fulton returned to America they began the construction of a full-size steamboat named the *Clermont,* in honor of the Chancellor's estate on the upper Hudson. Nick was drawn irresistibly to the shipyards on Paulus Hook where this craft was slowly taking shape. He saw the keel being laid for a vessel 133 feet in length, with an 18-foot beam and displacement of 160 tons. Doubtless he wondered at the masonry foundation for the needlessly exposed machinery amidships, and smiled at the two masts rising a bit higher than the 30-foot stack. He was disappointed to learn that the engine which was being installed had been

imported from Boulton and Watt in Birmingham.
Livingston might at least have awarded Nick the
contract to build the engine!

Roosevelt had his own industries to supervise and
therefore could not spend all of his time at Paulus
Hook. He was absent as the ship took its final form
and added its means of locomotion.

But he was very much on hand on the morning
of August 17, 1807, when every newspaper in New
York was blazoning the story of the trial run of the
Clermont from a Hudson River dock at Greenwich
Village. Nick was at least as curious as the thou-
sands of dirty urchins, young mechanics, tradesmen,

and professional people crowding every window, rooftop, alley, and street corner for a better look at the odd-looking vessel tied at the dock. Roosevelt found it difficult to push his way through the loafing sailors and street venders hawking their wares — the mob of idle curiosity seekers of both sexes who had come to cheer or jeer as the case might be. Not a few of them predicted that the boat would sink, or blow up in a great puff of white steam and crimson flame.

It was a motley and mixed crowd on the shore, but a very select one which was welcomed aboard the *Clermont* for the proposed trip to Albany.

Livingston and Fulton had been fastidious in their choice of shipboard companions, "the gentlemen elegant in spotless ruffles and professionally arranged hair," the women in their most stylish bonnets and dresses.

There was a delay during which Fulton made a few last-minute adjustments. But the crucial moment finally arrived. As the boat began to move steadily up the Hudson, there was sudden silence among the onlookers, followed by lusty cheers and the waving of many handkerchiefs.

Faster and faster moved this strange and cumbersome craft through the sunlit water. It would be a record run to Albany — a mere thirty-two hours against the usual five to nine days for a sailing vessel. Many aboard would report on that first really successful steamboat voyage, including Livingston and Fulton whose letters glow with self-satisfaction.

But standing on the dock, Nick Roosevelt experienced more misery than joy. The detail of the *Clermont* which stirred both his pride and his despair was its method of locomotion — those two great wheels, "over the sides," equipped with twelve paddles each, moving majestically through the water, throwing up rainbow spray as bright as on that dawn when he had first launched *his* model side-wheeler on the creek near Kingston.

Apparently neither Livingston nor Fulton felt any animosity toward Roosevelt at this time. In fact, quite the contrary! Livingston seldom suffered greatly from anything so unaristocratic as a guilty conscience, and probably never experienced a single sleepless night over his use of Roosevelt's invention. But as an ambitious man with great new projects in mind, he saw a way to make Nick useful. It would be better to have him as a partner in a fresh venture than to have him an envious enemy.

Fulton too preferred Nick's friendship to what might have become a feud. He agreed with Livingston that they might well use Roosevelt's talents — but as far from New York as possible. Why not on the great waterways beyond the Alleghenies where the Livingston-Fulton combine was already attempting to secure a monopoly on all future steamboat traffic on the Ohio and the Mississippi?

Fulton *was* a little worried about using other

men's inventions without credit, and was later to testify:

> I have no pretensions to be the first inventor of the steamboat. Hundreds of others have tried it and failed . . . That to which I claim an exclusive right is the so proportioning the boat to the power of the engine and the wheels of the boat . . . [as to assure] the maximum velocity attainable by the power . . .

Fulton added, "As to Mr. Roosevelt, I regard him as a noble-minded, intelligent man, and would do anything to serve him that I could."*

* The present book, presenting the case for Nicholas Roosevelt, "the forgotten man of the steamboat industry," should not be misinterpreted as an attack upon either Robert Fulton or Robert R. Livingston — both of whom were men of many virtues. Fulton's modest claim to have produced a workable proportion of engine to vessel is completely justified. Many inventors before Edison had experimented with electric lights, but Edison produced a globe that worked — and he deserves to be called "the inventor of the electric light." Fulton built the first *practical* steamboat, although various odd contraptions had crawled painfully over the waters of many lakes and rivers on both sides of the Atlantic. Furthermore, Fulton's unenvious admiration for Roosevelt is as typical of Fulton, as similar generosity was always typical of Roosevelt himself. It would be a great mistake for a biographer to be less generous than the principals, who, had they been men of smaller caliber, might easily have become mortal enemies.

It was probably through the good offices of Lydia's father — the architect-engineer Benjamin Henry Latrobe — that an agreement was now reached between the Fulton-Livingston interests and Nicholas Roosevelt, with a view to exploiting the potential traffic on the great Ohio-Mississippi waterway. But before any steamboat could be launched on western waters, it was necessary that an exploratory voyage be made — all the way from Pittsburgh to New Orleans — soundings to be taken of the depth of the water at frequent intervals for the entire 2000 miles, and every dangerous shoal and rapids studied with the greatest care.

Who was to make this voyage? Nicholas Roosevelt himself and his eighteen-year-old bride (who refused to be left behind)! Should Nick's findings be sufficiently hopeful, a steamboat would be built in a later year. And this vessel too would be under Roosevelt's command.

The reader may well imagine their excitement as Nick and Lydia made their way over the eastern mountains to the bustling frontier town of Pittsburgh in the spring of 1809 on a slightly delayed honeymoon which promised high adventure. Pittsburgh, where the Monongahela comes in from the south to meet the Allegheny pouring down from the northeast, is the source of the Ohio. In that year it was a town of about 4000 inhabitants, the "jumping-off place" for an ever-increasing horde of westward moving pioneers; a river port already emerging from its buckskin era to evolve into a busy, hopeful little metropolis. There were cotton weavers, glass blowers, brewers, tanners, and other primitive industrialists. But the principal interest of this key outpost was boat building and shipping — more than eighty shipwrights were continuously at work on new flatboats, keelboats, barges and similar vessels.

The first decision that Nick and Lydia had to make upon arrival concerned the sort of boat they should build for their months of exploration on the river.

The historic craft of this waterway were the Indian canoes which had glided over inland creeks and rivers for many hundreds of years. These were the swiftest, but most perishable cockleshells in which to dare the long journey ahead. They could be purchased for as little as three dollars each; but they could carry almost no provisions or equipment. Furthermore they offered no protection against the weather, against Indians, river pirates, or keelboatmen of the Mike Fink variety, roaring their boasts that they could: "Drink more whiskey and stay soberer, out-run, out-shoot, out-brag and out-fight ary a Salt River roarer in these here parts."

Pirogues, which were much like large canoes, could carry several tons of freight. They were sometimes fifty feet long and eight feet wide, and served the fur traders well. But this too would be a primitive way of travel for an eighteen-year-old girl accustomed to the comforts of civilization.

Keelboats and barges furnished other possibilities. These relatively commodious, slim, trim, and pointed craft could float downstream, and be poled laboriously back up the rivers against the current. But since Nick and Lydia wanted to make only the downstream voyage, their cost seemed disproportionate to the expedition's needs.

The least handsome, but most useful and comfortable craft, were the flatboats which were often forty to sixty feet in length, and ten to twenty feet in width. Constructed of squared timbers and heavy planks, with high gunwales, they could easily be protected from marauding Indians and river pirates and could carry a great tonnage while providing comfortable cabin space for all aboard. Flatboats were dismantled and sold for lumber at Natchez or New Orleans.

It didn't take Nick and Lydia long to decide that what they wanted to build was a flatboat. And Lydia — daughter of an architect — designed the living quarters.

Modern draftsmen insisting upon simplicity and

utility could take a leaf from Lydia's book. She wanted comfort and safety, plus privacy, and no cooking odors or noisy disturbance from the hired help. So she drew the plans for an admirable "house boat." Toward the prow was an extensive cabin for the pilot, three sailors, and the male cook. In this same room was a masonry fireplace where the wild turkeys, ducks, geese, and venison were to be roasted on a spit, the fish fried and all meals prepared.

To quote one of her own vivid letters, the larger apartment aft was "a huge box containing a com-

fortable bed room, dining room [and] pantry." Across the entire top of the boat ran a sun deck "flat, with seats and an awning."

It wasn't as sumptuous as the Latrobe house in Washington, or Laurel Hill, but it provided a snug floating home for the honeymooners from June to December of the year 1809. Whatever adventures lay ahead, they could face them more confidently from behind the heavy plank walls which no arrow or bullet could penetrate.

The forests were in full June foliage as the Roosevelt flatboat left its dock at Pittsburgh and swung into the current for its downstream pilgrimage.

Two sailors manned the "sweeps" — each handling one of these huge oars which extended on either side of the boat. A third sailor (or the pilot) tended the tiller — a somewhat similar oar, projecting from the stern.

Nick and Lydia sat comfortably beneath the awning on the flat upper deck enjoying the thrust of the water as they reached the confluence — the meeting point where the Allegheny joins the Monongahela to become the Ohio. As they rounded

the high promontory on the left, the town of Pittsburgh disappeared from view. Ahead lay 2000
miles of winding river and wilderness — the fertile
and untapped empire of sprawling mid-America.

Nick's moment of leisure on the observation deck
was brief. Taking his sounding line with its lead
weight, he was soon in the large rowboat testing
the depth of a fast piece of water he feared might
be too shallow for a steamboat. On rough maps
which he drew as the trip progressed he marked the
channels, registered their depths, and made frequent notes on the swiftness or sluggishness of the
current. Upon these findings much depended —
including his long-delayed opportunity to build a
side-wheel steamer.

Below Pittsburgh there were only two settle-
ments of any consequence on the Ohio. These
were Cincinnati, then a town of about 2500 inhabitants, and Louisville boasting perhaps half that
number. The Roosevelts stopped briefly at Cincinnati, where they were entertained by prominent
residents who wished them well. But not a single
Cincinnatian — merchant, lawyer, or hardy river-
man — could believe that Nick's ultimate project

would triumph. Yes, they had heard of the steamboat on the quiet Hudson, but such a craft would be worthless on these western rivers. It might go *downstream* with little trouble, but how could it ever *fight its way back* against such a current?

The citizens of Louisville were equally hospitable and equally dubious. There in full view lay a powerful piece of evidence — the dangerous Falls of the Ohio where the river plunged twenty-six feet in three miles through foam-flecked boulders and perilous cross currents. So formidable was this barrier to navigation that special local pilots were al-

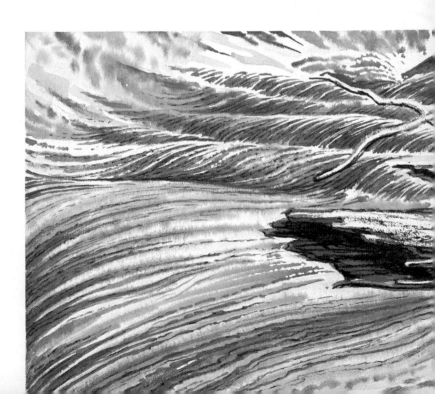

ways employed to help even the most experienced rivermen to take their flatboats, keelboats, and barges down the swirling rapids. Approximately eighteen hundred boats a year were so piloted.

Roosevelt realized that his envisioned steamboat journey might succeed or fail right here at the Falls. So he now spent three active weeks in Louisville sounding the depths and measuring the currents — often at considerable danger to his life.

Louisville in those days consisted principally of a single, mile-long street flanked by comfortable houses, and peopled by a particularly amiable populace — many of them from Virginia. During that three-week stopover, Lydia and Nick made friends with a number of the leading citizens.

When Roosevelt was finally convinced that he had gathered all possible information about the Falls, he, Lydia, the crew and a special pilot boarded the boat to make the breath-taking run down the steep rapids — all hands wondering how any *steamboat* could ever descend this cascade, much less fight its way up against the surging water.

Below the falls the sailing was again smooth on

La Belle Rivière (as the French poetically called it). "Nothing but woods, woods, woods, as far as the world extends" except for a few lonely settlers crying the usual greeting "Hello! The boat!" or the occasional raucous exchanges of rough good humor with rivermen on other boats they met or passed. On rare days they paused to fish bass and catfish or to hunt ducks or deer. Mostly, however, they plugged away steadily at their labors — mapping, sounding, and measuring the speed of the current.

So certain was Nicholas that they would again come this way that he sometimes took his men ashore to mine outcroppings of coal along the river-bank, leaving this black and potent fuel in gleaming piles, later to feed the fires beneath the boiler of the side-wheeler he was determined to build.

"Aren't we being a little too hopeful?" Lydia worried.

"Nonsense, my love! Next trip you'll be traveling in the cabin of a fine steamboat. What would you like to name her?"

Lydia looked up from her sewing and gazed off across the water.

"I think we should name her the *New Orleans* — that's our destination and the destination of almost every boat on the river."

"The *New Orleans* it will be" Nick promised.

According to Roosevelt's calculations they had floated some 1000 miles (981 by today's measurement) when they glided out one bright day onto the mighty Mississippi. For many miles below this confluence the water of the Ohio, clear and blue, refused to join the muddy current of the larger river, strewn with driftwood and stained with clay.

In time, however, the waters blended until no trace remained of La Belle Rivière. Now it was all one stream, the Father of Waters, bearing its great load of flotsam and of history — its memories of De Soto, Marquette, and La Salle — the treacherous, magnificent, mile-wide Mississippi winding its way to the Gulf. But here the dangers of snags, floating islands, and other hazards multiplied considerably. Here too the Indian menace increased.

Lydia recalled one occasion when "Mr. Roosevelt was aroused in the night by seeing two Indians in our sleeping room, calling for whiskey, when Mr.

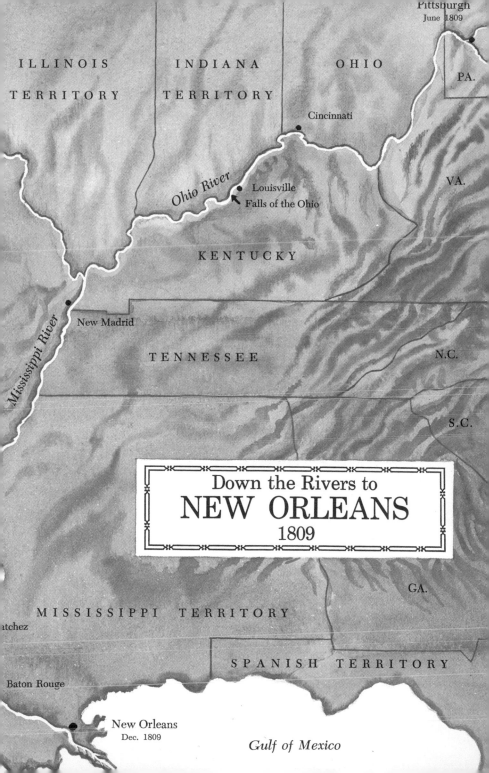

Pittsburgh
June 1809

ILLINOIS
TERRITORY

INDIANA
TERRITORY

OHIO

PA.

Cincinnati

Ohio River

Louisville
Falls of the Ohio

VA.

KENTUCKY

Mississippi River

New Madrid

TENNESSEE

N.C.

S.C.

Down the Rivers to
NEW ORLEANS
1809

GA.

MISSISSIPPI   TERRITORY

atchez

SPANISH   TERRITORY

Baton Rouge

New Orleans
Dec. 1809

Gulf of Mexico

Roosevelt had to get up and give it to them before he could induce them to leave the boat."

The Roosevelts had heard of the proposed model colony with wide streets and pleasant homes at New Madrid. But the reality was one of the sorriest-looking frontier villages on the entire river. They paused but briefly at this disheveled outpost, little realizing the part it would play on a subsequent voyage.

Southward now they floated, meeting no hazards worthy of mention, down hundreds of coiling miles of river — week upon drowsy week — gliding through a moist and steaming wilderness of cane-brakes and moss-draped forests where cougars sometimes screamed at night and waterbirds arose in clouds on whispering wings. They came at last to Natchez — one of the toughest, and most gracious towns on the Mississippi. The waterfront community, Natchez-under-the-hill, swarmed with river riffraff and their women. The town on top of the hill boasted some of the earliest mansions of the region, owned by Southern families of wealth and culture. Here the Roosevelts were again charmingly entertained. But the citizens of Natchez were as doubtful as those of Cincinnati and Louisville concerning the possibility of steamboat traffic on the river. They had only to step to the edge of the rose garden and point down at that treacherous, unpredictable stream to prove their point. No steamboat could ever breast such an irresistible force of water.

At Natchez, Roosevelt received a generous offer for his flatboat, and decided to accept it. Then with that trace of impulsive imbalance which sometimes motivated his actions, he started out with his bride and the crew in the large open rowboat on the downstream pull for New Orleans.

Lydia had enjoyed the flatboat trip. But she would never say the same for the final leg of this voyage, which lasted for nine unforgettable days and nights. Sometimes they slept in the boat itself, lying on buffalo robes spread over several trunks. Sometimes they slept on sandy beaches "hearing the alligators scratch on the sides [of the boat] . . . fancying, every moment, that something terrible might happen before morning."

Two nights were spent under roofs, one in the cabin of an old French Catholic couple, the second, on an evening of pouring rain, in a den of murderous characters in the village of Baton Rouge.

As Lydia later recalled:

> It was a miserable place at that time, with one wretched public house; yet we felt thankful that we had found a shelter from the storm. But when I was shewn into our sleeping room, I wished myself on board the boat. It was a forlorn little place opening out of the bar room, which was filled with tipsy men looking like cutthroats. The room had one window opening into a stable yard, but which had neither shutters nor fastenings. Its furniture was a single chair and dirty bed. We threw our cloaks on the bed and laid down to rest, but not to sleep, for the fighting and the noise in the bar room prevented that. We rose at the dawn of day and reached the boat, feeling thankful we had not been murdered in the night.

Reaching New Orleans at last, fatigued and yet elated, they had little time to accept hospitality before catching the first ship ready to sail for the eastern seaboard. Wrote Lydia of that ocean trip:

We had a terrible voyage of a month, with a sick captain. The yellow fever was on board. A passenger, a nephew of General Wilkinson, died with it. Mr. Roosevelt and myself were taken off the ship by a pilot boat and landed at Old Point Comfort [Virginia]. From thence we went to New York by stage, reaching there the middle of January, 1810, after an absence of nine months.

One might have thought that Roosevelt and his wife would have had enough of the Ohio and the Mississippi, of Indians, cutthroats, and yellow fever, of alligators and snags and tropic downpours. Far from it. Both were as eager as ever to build a steamboat in Pittsburgh and take it triumphantly down river to New Orleans.

6

First Steamboat on Western Waters

LIVINGSTON and Fulton were pleased with Roosevelt's report and immediately incorporated the Ohio Steamboat Navigation Company, with Nick as its western agent. But the Chancellor was still wily and dictatorial, hedging this partnership agreement with slippery legal phrases. He insisted that Robert Fulton draw the plans for the boat (although Fulton knew nothing of many of the special problems involved). And he particularly cautioned Roosevelt against extravagance.

As Nick explained to Lydia after this first conference, the terms were probably the best he could obtain from Livingston, and he had little choice save to accept. However, he promised his wife that once they were in Pittsburgh, a satisfying 320 miles west of New York City, he would let neither Livingston nor Fulton interfere disastrously with the construction of the *New Orleans*. This time there would be no argument concerning the obvious necessity for "wheels over the sides." Furthermore, Nick himself would design and build the powerful marine engine with a 34-inch cylinder — strong enough to spin those giant wheels on any voyage.

The Roosevelts again crossed the Alleghenies, and soon were settled in comfortable quarters at the Forks of the Ohio. The boatyard and foundry were located on the eastern bank of the Monongahela about a mile above the Point, "immediately under a lofty bluff called Boyd's Hill."

Within a matter of weeks tall white pines were being cut farther up the Monongahela, to be rafted down to the shipyard, where they were laboriously sawed into planks and timbers. The keel was soon being laid for a vessel to be 116 feet in length, with a 20-foot beam and an estimated displacement of over 300 tons.

There was one feature in the Fulton drawings which disturbed Roosevelt profoundly. Nick was convinced that any river boat on the Ohio would need a sufficiently shallow draft to run the Falls, and yet Fulton's plans called for such depth in the hull as to make a safe passage most unlikely.

With Fulton and Livingston far from the scene of action, Roosevelt wisely decided to reduce the draft of the vessel and make such other minor changes as he thought necessary.

There were excellent local shipwrights for building the hull and the superstructure. But no one in Pittsburgh in that era knew anything about building or installing a steam engine. For this purpose Roosevelt had to import mechanics from New York and New Jersey. Also, since there was no copper rolling mill or boiler works west of the Alleghenies, the huge and cumbersome copper boiler had to be freighted by ox team over the steep mountain roads from the east — a slow and painful journey.

Nick reveled in building the great new engine. He was always on hand to encourage the men fashioning the valves, hand-filing the interior of the cylinder, or working on the "sun-and-planet" gears whereby the engine's power was transmitted to the paddle wheels. Because so many materials had to be imported over those treacherous mountain trails, the work went slowly and the expenses mounted alarmingly.

Livingston and Fulton, who were having their own financial difficulties in the east, wrote many letters — first of caution, then of increasing anger. Roosevelt did everything he could to reduce expenses, but they continued to soar.

Eventually, when it became apparent that the little steamboat could not be completed for less than

$38,000, the old Chancellor wrote such wrathful letters that they permanently impaired his relationship with his western agent.

Another near-disaster came one stormy night when the Monongahela rose to flood stage in a matter of hours, lifting the incompleted *New Orleans* from its dry dock, and threatening to send the vessel on its downstream journey months before it was ready. Nick and his workmen rushed to the shipyards, tossed cables to the deck, and by the narrowest margin saved it from destruction.

Despite Livingston and high water, however, the work continued, until, at long last — *there stood the vessel,* ready for the launching.

Pittsburgh had proved a friendly town during the eighteen months consumed in constructing and fitting the steamboat. However, there were many men who still scoffed at "the fool-hardy notion of running a boat by fire," deriding the whole idea as "mechanical insanity." Meanwhile the women of the town were incensed by a more feminine aspect of the trip which they considered "utter folly, if not absolute madness." Their sense of propriety was outraged by the fact that Lydia, who was about to have a baby, insisted upon accompanying her husband on this wild excursion down the Ohio and the Mississippi — through 2000 miles of wilderness to New Orleans.

Neither Lydia nor Nicholas paid much attention to the dire predictions of their Pittsburgh neighbors. In fact, all this criticism slid off their backs as readily as water sheered from the prow of the *New Orleans* when on October 20, 1811, this strange craft with its tall smokestack and slapping paddle wheels pulled out into the Monongahela. Its blue hull was as vivid as the autumn sky — startling against the forest background of crimson maples, leather-brown oaks, and golden water elms.

A large crowd, including all the doubting males and disapproving females, had gathered to watch the launching — a few offering silent prayers, and others denouncing this "invention of the Devil."

But Nicholas and Lydia remained calm and assured. Nick ordered the helmsman to head upstream, just to prove to the assembled multitude that the *New Orleans* could buck the current. It made a wide and graceful circuit, then turned downstream again on its proper course and came sweeping triumphantly past the crowd on the shore. The effect was as dramatic as Nick had hoped it would be. "Shout after shout rent the air, and handkerchiefs were waved, and hats thrown up by way of 'God speed.' "

Soon the vessel passed the Point, and shortly thereafter disappeared behind the bluff on the far shore to begin its descent of the Ohio.

Lydia Roosevelt, more than sixty years later, could still remember every detail of the boat and the trip — for this undoubtedly was one of the most exciting moments of her life.*

On this river steamer there was ample room for passengers, crew, and as many as sixty or seventy additional persons desiring a short excursion. Toward the bow of the boat there was space for many tons of cargo, the machinery was amidships, and most of the cabins were aft. Ruggedly constructed to take the shock of snags and reefs, the

---

* Lydia's half brother, J. H. B. Latrobe, drawing almost entirely upon Lydia's memories and letters, delivered a lecture to the Maryland Historical Society which has been preserved in a pamphlet entitled *The First Steamboat Voyage on the Western Waters* (Baltimore, 1871). This relatively rare and valuable bit of Americana is almost the only primary source material available on this first voyage of the *New Orleans* and is the basis for most of the facts found in this chapter.

New Orleans was overly heavy for Ohio River cruising, but would serve admirably in the deepwater New Orleans-Natchez trade for which it had been built.

Besides Lydia and Nick, there was "a captain, an engineer named Baker, Andrew Jack, the pilot, six hands, two female servants, a man waiter, a cook, and an immense Newfoundland dog, named Tiger. Thus equipped, the *New Orleans* began the voyage which changed the relations of the West, — which may almost be said to have changed its destiny."

Lydia — still a young woman of but twenty years — had previously made this same trip by flatboat. But this could not dim for her the romance of the new adventure. She and Nicholas were "too much excited to sleep." So they "passed the greater part of the night on deck," watching by starlight the darkly forested hills sweep majestically away behind them as the *New Orleans* progressed smoothly at an even eight to ten miles an hour. The steady throb of the big engine and the uniformity of the speed gave confidence not only to the Roosevelts. It also "quieted the nervous apprehension" of the crew. The pilot was delighted with the ease with which the vessel steered — and all hands found their cabins comfortable and cool.

After snatching a few hours sleep, Lydia and Nick were up again to greet the sun. Villagers of a little settlement they were passing called cheerfully. And from the deck went answering cheers across the water. The new steamboat was well on its way, manned by "as jolly a set as ever floated on the Ohio."

Two days out of Pittsburgh the *New Orleans* cast anchor briefly at Cincinnati. Many friends whom the Roosevelts had acquired on the previous voyage came to the waterfront to marvel at this "eighth wonder of the world." But they still were doubtful: "Well, you are as good as your word; you have visited us in a steamboat," they admitted; "but we see you for the last time. Your boat may go *down* the river; but as to coming up it, the very idea is an absurd one."

"You'll see us again, and soon," Nick promised.

The *New Orleans* remained at anchor only long enough to take on a supply of wood, then headed downstream. It arrived at Louisville on the fourth night out of Pittsburgh — sailing time, sixty-four hours.

Lydia remembered it as a midnight of brilliant moonlight. "It was as light as day almost, and no one on board had retired. The roar of the escaping steam . . . roused the population, and, late as it was, crowds came rushing to the bank of the river to learn the cause of the unwonted uproar."

Some citizens thought that the Comet of 1811 — already a cause of great anxiety among the superstitious — had actually fallen into the river, creating

the ominous hiss of steam echoing over the water.

Next morning many acquaintances came aboard, but most of them were as dubious as the inhabitants of Cincinnati. Their "congratulations at having descended the river" were accompanied by "regrets that it was the first and last time a steamboat would be seen above the Falls of the Ohio."

Roosevelt could see at a glance that the Falls were in no condition to float such a vessel as the *New Orleans*. The river was at a much lower stage than it had been during his previous visit, and many boulders then covered with water were now exposed. There was no alternative except to cast anchor and wait for higher water.

In many ways, however, this pause in their journey was fortunate and pleasant for all concerned.

(*Audubon, the artist and ornithologist, had brought his young wife Lucy to Louisville a few years earlier. They had arrived "utter strangers" but had discovered that "the matrons acted like mothers" to Lucy while "the husbands and sons were friends and companions" to Audubon himself.*)

Nicholas and Lydia were now treated with similar kindness. These same matrons openly expressed their hope that there would be no rise in the river until Lydia's baby was born in one of the comfortable homes now offering her shelter. For Nick's sake, Lydia wanted no delay and had fully expected to give birth to her baby aboard the *New Orleans*. But she did welcome the luxury of a four-poster bed in one of the large and airy chambers of a newfound friend.

Meanwhile a great banquet was given in honor of these intrepid Argonauts. The Roosevelts, not to be outdone, prepared a similar feast aboard the *New Orleans*.

The festivities were at their height when suddenly deep rumblings were heard, accompanied by a "very perceptible motion" of the vessel. All the guests had a single and horrifying thought: "The *New Orleans* had escaped from her anchor, and was drifting toward the Falls, to the certain destruction of all on board."

Instantly there was a rush to the upper deck where the company found "that, instead of drifting towards the Falls of the Ohio, the *New Orleans* was making good headway up the river and would soon leave Louisville in the distance down stream." The guests were surprised and delighted, and at least partly convinced that Roosevelt might be right about the rosy future of steamboating on the Ohio.

Nick's first experiment of this kind had worked so successfully that he now planned a more impressive demonstration. Since the river remained at a very low stage, he decided to take an excursion upstream to Cincinnati and return, leaving Lydia in comfort in Louisville. The vessel performed perfectly on this round trip, and the Cincinnatians, who had been so doubtful, now expressed "unbounded confidence."

After returning to Louisville where neither the expected baby nor the rise in the Ohio seemed immediately imminent, Nick visited his wife each day, then spent several hours taking soundings in the channel through the cascade.

One day he was amazed to see forty brawny rivermen poling a 95-foot barge *up* the rapids — straining every muscle to move the great boat inch by inch against the current. When the loaded vessel was safely at anchor beside the *New Orleans*, Nick was pleased and proud to have its young captain ask to come aboard.

Shreve

As Roosevelt immediately realized, this barge owner was a remarkable man. His name — Henry Miller Shreve — rang a remote bell in Nick's mind, for Shreve was already mildly famous along the river, having made a modest fortune in transporting furs from St. Louis to Pittsburgh and in moving lead downstream from the Galena mines. He stood five feet eleven — a slight, very strong, quiet and highly intelligent Quaker, who at twenty-six years of age still wore the traditional knee breeches and broad hat of his sect, and used the courteous and quaint "thee" and "thou" he had learned from his

parents. Mild and friendly as Shreve was, Nick noticed that his forty tough rivermen treated him with great respect and moved swiftly to do his bidding.

Shreve was fascinated by the *New Orleans* and examined every aspect of its machinery with keen and comprehending eyes. As Nick told Lydia, Shreve was a man who would have a steamboat of his own one of these days — and a baby too, he added, since Henry's young wife Mary was also expecting a child this very month. Nick wished that the barge captain could have prolonged his stay, but like any young husband he was eager to hurry home to be with his wife when the baby arrived at their home in Brownsville on the Monongahela.

After the barge moved up the Ohio, time hung heavy over the *New Orleans*. The long-delayed rise in the river made the crew restless, while the delayed birth of the baby gave Nick even greater apprehension. As though to emphasize the anxiety of that strange year, news of possible war with England was on every tongue, and the very heavens seemed ominous.

> There was a dull, misty sky without a cloud — a leaden atmosphere that weighed upon the spirits, and the meaning of which would have been better understood at Naples under the shadow of Vesuvius, than on the banks of the Ohio. The sun, when it rose, looked like a globe of red hot iron, whose color brightened at noon, to resume the same look when it sank below the horizon . . . The air was still and heated; and a sense of weariness was the characteristic of the hours as they wore slowly by. At last, when a nervous impatience affected every one on board, it was

announced, one morning, that there had been
a rise in the river during the night.

But for Nicholas there was another announce-
ment which touched him far more deeply. During
that same night Lydia had borne them a son; and
mother and child were doing beautifully in the care
of the kind friends who had taken her into their
home.

Each day Lydia grew stronger, and each day the
river continued to rise. Finally, in the last week of
November, Nick discovered that the depth of water
in the shallowest part of the Falls "exceeded by
five inches the draught of the boat."

That furnished a very narrow margin, but the rise
in the river had ceased. It was now or never,
Nicholas Roosevelt told himself. He conferred with
Lydia, and together they decided, quite literally, to
"take the plunge." Dauntless Lydia was once again
determined to live or die with her husband, and
not to wait to join the boat below the Falls.

Husband and wife, with their little son in her
arms, stood side by side as the special pilot assumed
his place at the bow. The order was given to up-

anchor, and steam was crowded into the boiler until the safety valve screeched its warning. The boat made a wide circuit to enter the Indiana channel on the far side of the river. Then the vessel began its swift descent. To make steering possible it was necessary to have the boat moving far faster than the current. Now the great paddle wheels whirled more swiftly than ever before, adding two trails of froth on the water. While the crowd of spectators held its breath for fear that all aboard would perish, the good ship *New Orleans* fairly flew over the turbulent river.

> Instinctively, each one on board now grasped the nearest object . . . Black ledges of rock appeared, only to disappear as the *New Orleans* flashed by them. The waters whirled and eddied, and threw their spray upon the deck, as a more rapid descent caused the vessel to pitch forward to what at times seemed inevitable destruction. Not a word was spoken . . . Even the great Newfoundland dog seemed affected by the apprehension of danger, and came and crouched at Mrs. Roosevelt's feet . . . The tension . . . was too great to be long sustained.

Fortunately, the passage was soon made . . . with feelings of profound gratitude to the Almighty.

Safe in the deep and quiet waters below the Falls, the *New Orleans* rounded to, and cast anchor to let the special pilot go ashore, and to give all aboard a short rest before continuing their journey down the Ohio on the second leg of their great adventure.

Nick and Lydia had but a few hours to enjoy their sense of accomplishment and relief. They had fully expected clear sailing ahead once they had navigated this dangerous cataract. But even while they lay at anchor a new terror assailed them.

"There was still the same leaden sky — the same dim sun." And now the boat was abruptly shaken as though by a great and unseen hand. Everyone rushed to the deck, babbling questions which no one could answer. "The effect was as though the vessel had been in motion and had suddenly grounded. The cable shook and trembled, and many on board experienced for the moment a nausea resembling sea sickness."

Thus began a period which Lydia called "those

days of horror" and which the whole frontier would remember as "The Year of the Great Shakes." These were the first tremors of the New Madrid Earth-quake, which shook the mid-continent as a terrier shakes a rat — the most violent earthquake to strike the Midwest within the memory of man.

All night long, and for many days and nights to come, the shocks continued at irregular intervals. During the daytime when the boat was in motion, the jarring of the machinery and the monotonous slap-slapping of the paddle wheels prevented the voyagers from detecting any but the most severe shocks. But there was one on board able to sense every tremor, and that was the big dog Tiger. He "prowled about, moaning and growling; and when he came and placed his head on Mrs. Roosevelt's lap, it was a sure sign of a commotion of more than usual violence."

Brave though she was, Lydia would later admit that she "lived in a constant fright, unable to sleep or sew, or read."

One of the most uncanny aspects of this ghostly journey through shrouded days and starless nights was the silence on board the *New Orleans*. Except for the noise of the machinery and the paddle wheels, a funereal hush hung over the vessel.

> No one seemed disposed to talk; and when there was any conversation, it was carried on in whispers, almost . . . Orders were given in low tones; and the usual cheerful, "aye, aye, sir," of the sailors was almost inaudible . . . Flat boats and barges were passed, whose crews, instead of bandying river wit, as they had done . . . uttered no word as the *New Orleans* went by.

It was necessary each day to go ashore for fuel — sometimes to bring aboard the coal which Roosevelt and his men had mined on the previous trip, but more often to cut wood. Even though this chance to stretch their legs had been considered the treat of the day, the men now toiled silently. "And if the earth shook, as it often did . . . the uplifted axe was suspended, or placed quietly on the log, and the men stared at each other until it ceased."

Indians and squatters alike viewed the steamship with increasing fear. Seeing sparks flying from its tall smokestack, they connected this evil magic with the comet which so recently had crossed the sky;

and hearing the rumble of the engines and the hiss of the escaping steam, they were certain that the vessel was also the cause of the continuing earthquake. Some fled in fear. Others stood on the shore quietly cursing the boat. At one small settlement across the river from the William Henry Harrison farm, a settler, frightened out of his wits by the boat, went screaming to warn his neighbors that "the British are coming down the river"! At another pinpoint village a loafer, loaded with his own corn whiskey, looked up to see "a terrible contraption" emerging from the river mist. To his startled wife

he yelled, "It's the Devil floatin' down to New Orleans on a sawmill."

The tremors intensified as the steamboat left the Ohio to risk its existence on the vastly flooded Mississippi. And here the Chickasaws — who had heard by Indian grapevine of this ferocious monster coming to destroy them — decided to demolish the wicked Manitou. Filling a huge war canoe with their bravest warriors, they lay in ambush among the half-submerged trees, and darted out so swiftly and silently that no one aboard the *New Orleans* was aware of the attackers until they were almost abreast of the boat. Then the silence was broken by the bloodcurdling war cries of the determined savages.

Roosevelt was a courageous man. However, concerned for the safety of Lydia and the baby, and well aware that his little crew was far outnumbered, he decided against a pitched battle. Instead he gave the signal for "full steam ahead." Thus began the "first steamboat race on the Mississippi."

The Indians were too busy plying their paddles to seize their weapons; and they had rightly concluded that the only way to destroy this great

"Penelore" or "fire canoe" was to board it in strength, kill the palefaces and then sink the boat. Bronze muscles rippled as the pencil-slim canoe seemed for a time to be gaining on the steamboat. But as fresh fuel was added and additional steam poured into the engine, the *New Orleans* pulled slowly but surely beyond the range of any arrow or bullet. From the war canoe, now falling astern, came howls of frustration as from wolves deprived of their prey.

As though one such experience were not enough for the day, the evening held still another surprise. Roosevelt and Lydia had retired to their cabin for the night and were still talking about the Chickasaw raid when they were startled by screams and a great commotion on deck. Snatching up the first weapon at hand — which happened to be a sword — Nick rushed from the cabin, prepared to defend the boat from Indians, pirates, or boarders of any variety.

What he discovered was an enemy more deadly than Indians — a raging fire. The December nights had become chill, and too hot a fire had been kept in the stove in the forward cabin. Green wood, piled near the stove to dry, had been ignited, and the fire had then spread to the wood paneling of the cabin itself. Alone on the dark and flooded river, all on board might have perished if the fire had burned the boat to the water line. Quickly organizing a bucket brigade, Roosevelt directed his panic-stricken crew with the efficiency of a fire chief until the last ember was quenched. The hull and the cabins to the rear were undamaged, but the forward cabin had become a charred wreck.

To add to all their other difficulties, the earthquake had changed the channel of the Mississippi

so drastically that all of Nick's maps and soundings were useless. The pilot and the crew — all experienced river men — were as puzzled as Roosevelt himself as they passed landmarks they had never seen before, or sped through new "chutes" cut by the torrent across flooded oxbows. So many banks had been undermined by the flood that tying up to the shore was an invitation to suicide since tall trees constantly toppled into the river from these eroding shores.

To lessen the danger of being crushed by falling trees, Roosevelt hit upon the plan of anchoring at

night at the downstream tip of large islands, thus also protecting the boat from the mass of flotsam hurtling along on the brown flood. On one such night — after a fairly restful day — Lydia thought they all might get their first sound sleep since leaving Louisville. But all night long there were such bumps and jars and scrapings that Mrs. Roosevelt was reminded of their night among the alligators. This was too far north for alligators, however, and the objects hitting the boat were so heavy that they jarred the 300-ton vessel as though it were attacked by a herd of angry elephants.

At first light, everyone hit the deck, where to their surprise they discovered that the big island had entirely disappeared during the night, washed away by the rampaging river. What they had been hearing and feeling in the darkness was the disintegrating island — uprooted trees and mountains of driftwood torn from the now-vanished bit of land. At first everyone believed that the *New Orleans* too must have been carried downstream. But landmarks on the shore showed them to be in precisely the position of the previous evening. They tried to lift the anchor but found it so hopelessly enmeshed in heavy trees submerged beneath the water that they had to cut the cable to free the boat.

Perhaps the most harrowing experience of this trip was a brief stop at what had been New Madrid. Much of the town had simply vanished, some of the houses sinking into twenty-five feet of water. The pitiful survivors begged to be taken aboard the *New Orleans*, but delays had so reduced the boat's provisions that they were scarcely sufficient to feed those already on board.

"Painful as it was, there was no choice but to turn a deaf ear to the cries of the terrified inhabitants of the doomed town."

After days that seemed like weeks, the *New Orleans* finally emerged from the earthquake area, and once again Nick and Lydia could enjoy the enormous flocks of migrating ducks and geese and swans now moving south along this great central flyway. In those days, brilliant little parakeets were everywhere, and the now all-but-extinct whooping crane was not a novelty. The dismal hooting of owls and the angry scream of the catamounts in the canebrakes mingled with the night-long calling of the whippoorwills to produce a wild symphony — brooding and beautiful, but sometimes frightening.

They came at last to Natchez where on the 200-foot bluff new mansions were already arising. Both the tough waterfront and the hill were thick with spectators — all looking at the very first steamboat they had ever seen. But at this dramatic moment the engineer unwittingly furnished a moment of anticlimax. Knowing that the vessel would be

Natchez

docking for several days at Natchez he had let the fires burn low under the boiler, so that when Roosevelt signaled for what he hoped would be a graceful landing, circling downstream to curve upstream again to the dock, the vessel was powerless to stem the current.

Had the *New Orleans* come all this way to fail them now? The crowds were silent with disappointment, and Roosevelt was embarrassed. But new fuel and a fresh head of steam soon retrieved the steamboat's honor. The big engine again took hold, the paddle wheels began to turn, and the *New Orleans*, responding with its usual dependability, steamed steadily against the current to the landing while thousands on the shore and on the hill cheered the performance.

Nick and Lydia were again entertained, and with an added touch of romance to cap their voyage. During the trip Nicholas Baker had been promoted to the captaincy. But he had also found time quietly to woo Mrs. Roosevelt's pretty maid. The happy couple were married in one of the gracious homes on the hill as a fitting climax to the whole adventure.

The *New Orleans* arrived at the port for which it was named on January 10, 1812, and we can only conjecture what next transpired. Apparently Chancellor Livingston had conveyed to his younger brother Edward Livingston some of the annoyance he felt over the cost of building this first steamboat on western waters. And Edward, who had been living in New Orleans for several years, may have been abrupt or tactless in his treatment of Nicholas Roosevelt.

Edward, who was some eighteen years younger than the Chancellor, was at least as stubborn, aristocratic and overbearing as his older brother and possibly even more brilliant. He had been Mayor of New York and would eventually become Secretary of State under President Jackson. Just now he was the most formidable lawyer in New Orleans, numbering among his many clients the pirate Lafitte brothers. If anyone could defend the Fulton-Livingston monopoly on the lower Mississippi it was Edward Livingston.

Roosevelt had just completed a history-making and heroic trip. What he expected — at the very least — was a pleasant welcome from this business associate. What he got instead was doubtless very different. Ingratitude coupled with injustice is hard for any man to bear — particularly one as sensitive, proud and talented as Nicholas Roosevelt. Nick probably realized that he might outlive the Chancellor and Robert Fulton — both ailing.* But at this southern port he would always be at the mercy of this younger dictator.

Nick made one of those quick decisions which were so characteristic of his nature. He simply resigned command, turning the boat over to Edward Livingston and Captain Baker; and with Lydia and the baby, left by sea for New York. Once back in the East he apparently sold all of his property, liquidated his debts, and, with what remained, moved with his little family to the pleasant town of Skaneateles in the beautiful Finger Lake region of the state of New York. Here he and Lydia raised a happy family and lived in modest comfort well into their eighties, looking out over more tranquil waters.

---

* Robert R. Livingston died in 1813. Robert Fulton followed him in 1815.

A short postscript should be added to this chapter to comfort the reader and the descendants of Nicholas and Lydia.

The Chancellor lived long enough to learn that he had not wasted his $38,000 in building the *New Orleans*. In its very first year plying the Natchez–New Orleans route, it earned approximately $20,000 (or more than half the cost of construction). Before it went aground on July 14, 1814, near Baton Rouge it had more than repaid the Livingstons. Even following that disaster, its engine, boiler and other machinery were in such excellent condition that they were salvaged to be used in a second steamship also called the *New Orleans*.

Nicholas Roosevelt was further vindicated in his lifelong assertion that it was he who had invented "wheels over the sides." In the year 1814 he applied for and was granted a United States patent for this device which seemed to be in conflict with a patent for which Fulton had applied in 1809. On sober second thought the patent office gave the laurels to Roosevelt.

Although the great cost of litigation made it impossible for Roosevelt ever to defend this patent in court, Roger B. Taney (later Chief Justice of the Supreme Court) was absolutely certain of the legality of Roosevelt's claim, and was ready, personally, to defend it had Nicholas so desired.

A final feather in the cap of this "forgotten" man was the pageant held in his honor at Pittsburgh one hundred years after the launching of the *New Orleans*. A replica of that vessel, plus some fifty other festooned river steamers, produced a parade of packets never duplicated before or since. Among the honored guests were President William Howard Taft and descendants of the Livingston, Fulton, and Fitch families. Alice Roosevelt Longworth, great-great-granddaughter of Nick's brother James J. led the Roosevelt delegation.

The event evoked the deep nostalgia all rivermen feel concerning river steamers. And, for the moment at least, America was aware of those two pioneers — Nicholas and Lydia — who braved the Falls of the Ohio, Chickasaw warriors, earthquake, fire and flood to launch the most romantic era in American history — the era of the steamboat on western waters.

7

Shreve Clears the Channel

DURING the next three years Henry Miller Shreve (for whom Shreveport, Louisiana is named) continued to operate his barges on the round-trip run to New Orleans. But his mind was constantly upon steamboats. They certainly appeared to be the logical answer to the dangerous, toilsome upstream navigation by oars, poles, sails and human towropes (which the straining bargemen called *cordelles*).

Several serious difficulties forced even the courageous Shreve to bide his time, however. A steamboat was an expensive craft to build, and none so far had proved powerful enough to make the upriver run from New Orleans to Pittsburgh. A more formidable barrier was the Fulton-Livingston monopoly which made it illegal for a steamboat of any other company to violate Louisiana waters or to tie up at New Orleans.

During this time the Fulton-Livingston interests (now dominated by Edward Livingston) built three more steamboats, the *Vesuvius,* the *Etna,* and the second *New Orleans.* None of these vessels could breast a strong current, and on only a few occasions did they venture farther upriver than Natchez.

A little sternwheeler, the *Comet,* built by Daniel French in Shreve's home port of Brownsville on the Monongahela, descended to New Orleans in the spring of 1814, but proved no better than the other boats in bucking fast water. It was soon dismantled and the engine sold for use in a cotton factory.

Shreve, however, was not discouraged. He was sure that more efficient steamboats could be built, and he was equally certain that Edward Livingston could not permanently block steam traffic on the Mississippi. In anticipation of future trouble, Shreve hired the only lawyer in New Orleans not in the pay of the Fulton-Livingston combine, a brilliant and honest man named A. L. Duncan. He then poled his way homeward on his barge to become the captain of Daniel French's new steamboat, the *Enterprise*. On December 1, 1814, he started the long down-river run, reaching New Orleans in fourteen days.

Edward Livingston immediately began a legal move to seize the boat. But General Andrew Jackson — famous hard-fighting Old Hickory himself — told Livingston he would have to wait his turn. Jackson, who had just arrived in New Orleans with a tattered army of Indian fighters, was facing the test of his life against a huge army of British soldiers, sailors, and marines anchored in a flotilla off Lake Borgne to the east of the city. In this final phase of the War of 1812 there was a strong possibility that New Orleans might be captured and even burned.

The arrival of the *Enterprise* at this moment was a godsend. Jackson ordered Shreve to head upstream to see if he could find several long-overdue keelboats loaded with urgently needed ammunition. North of Natchez he found them; hitched them on behind, and rushed them down to New Orleans. He had not only fulfilled his mission, he had driven his

steamboat 654 miles in six and one half days.

Delighted with Shreve's performance, Jackson now proposed a far more dangerous assignment.

"Captain Shreve," he said, "I understand that you are a man who will always do what you undertake. Can you pass the British batteries on the river nine miles below, and with your steamer bear supplies to Fort St. Philip?"

Shreve knew that those heavy English guns not only dominated the entire width of the river, but were capable of blowing his vessel to splinters. He immediately agreed, however. On his boat he swiftly built a bulwark of cotton bales, held in place by heavy hooks, thus constructing the oddest floating fortress ever seen. Toward evening, when all the needed supplies had been stowed aboard, he dropped down the river. Fortunately it was a dark night. The engine was closed down so that no warning sound could reach the ears of the British sentries. Fort St. Philip received its desperately needed supplies, and Shreve began his far more difficult ascent against the current.

This time there was no chance to muffle the engine or the wheel. The British guns opened fire as the *Enterprise* labored by, but through good fortune and poor marksmanship only a few spent balls imbedded themselves harmlessly in the cotton bales.*

Shreve had now become a hero in besieged New Orleans, but he had no time to bask in his new popularity. He was much too busy freighting arms and other supplies to the plantations seven and one half miles south of the city where Jackson was im-

---

* In contrast to the scarcity of material on Nicholas Roosevelt, there are several books on Henry Miller Shreve. One of the best is *Master of the Mississippi* by Florence L. Dorsey (Houghton Mifflin, 1941). Grateful acknowledgment is hereby given for its use as a reference book in checking several specific facts in this chapter.

provising a defensive line built of the only materials available, cotton bales and mud. The British, facing the same difficulties, were using hundreds of barrels of sugar to bolster their defenses. Despite the arrival of hardy frontiersmen from Kentucky and Tennessee, the odds were still strongly against the Americans, many of whom lacked even a musket or a rifle. It seemed all but incredible that the outnumbered, outgunned Americans could hope to stand against the thousands of well-trained, magnificently equipped, smartly uniformed redcoats and the sturdy Highlanders in their kilts (piped into battle to the sound of bagpipes).

This was the moment for every patriot in New Orleans to give his utmost. Many quarrels were momentarily forgotten in the crisis. Jackson had called the Lafitte brothers scoundrels and pirates, but he now accepted their help in the defense of New Orleans. Edward Livingston served as Jackson's aide-de-camp at the battle front. And Henry Miller Shreve, Quaker though he was, begged to be allowed to fight for his country. Jackson hesitated to risk so valuable a man, but finally consented. Shreve had his wish and served bravely in Colonel

Humphrey's battery, personally taking charge of gun No. 6, "a long twenty-four-pounder." Thus Shreve and his enemy Livingston faced Wellington's veterans as they appeared in flashing array out of the mist that never-to-be-forgotten morning of January 8, 1815. And together they fought all that bloody day to help our buckskin-clad frontiersmen inflict the most overwhelming and decisive defeat England had sustained on this continent since the Battle of Yorktown.

One might have thought that comradeship in arms would mellow Edward Livingston in his dealings with Henry Miller Shreve. But such was not his nature.

After Shreve had completed many additional missions for Jackson in the aftermath of the battle, the *Enterprise* was released from government service, but almost immediately was seized by Livingston. Attorney Duncan arranged for bail, and after some delay and inconvenience, Shreve again headed up the river with a full cargo and several passengers.

This was a test run which the captain secretly doubted he could achieve — the upriver trip from New Orleans to Louisville. Above Natchez it became apparent that the *Enterprise* — like all its predecessors — could not force its way against the heaviest currents. Fortunately the Mississippi was greatly flooded, and Shreve shrewdly guided his vessel into the more placid waters flanking the river, skimming easily over the flooded fields and marshes. Thus he avoided most of the turbulent currents of the river itself. By such maneuvers he reached Louisville in twenty-five days and Brownsville in fifty-four. Inhabitants of the upper Ohio were lyrical in their praise and bursting with new confidence concerning the coming steamboat era. But no one knew so thoroughly as Shreve that the upstream problem had not really been whipped, and never would be unless an entirely new type of steamboat was constructed.

Captain Shreve was a quiet but forceful man. From the day he launched his first keelboat he had always found it easier to express himself in action than in words. His fertile brain was seething with new ideas for a radically different type of river steamer, but he was unable to convince his good friend and neighbor Daniel French that these "wild notions" were anything but fantasy.

If French would not build the boat, then Shreve would build it himself. Investing every cent he had saved (plus all that he could borrow), he now began to build the *Washington* — a completely new concept in engine design, hull, and superstructure; a boat so strange that no one believed it would even stay afloat.

In August 1815 the timbers of the *Washington* were still "growing in the woods." Less than a year later, accompanied by the dire predictions of almost everyone who watched the launching, this first truly modern river steamer slid down the ways into the river to float as gracefully as a swan upon the water.

The major prediction of the onlookers was that it would tip over, because it was the first river boat to have two decks, topped by the pilot house. Its draft was several feet shallower than in the Fulton-Livingston boats, thus making it seem even more top-heavy than it really was, but allowing it to float with ease over shoals where the earlier boats would have grounded.

One hundred and forty-eight feet in length,

measuring 403 tons, the *Washington* was by far the
largest steamboat afloat on western waters. The
cabins were placed between the decks and were
luxuriously decorated and furnished. The main
cabin was sixty feet in length. There was a commodious bar for gentlemen passengers, and several
"handsome private rooms."

But perhaps the most radical departure from all
previous steamers was the engine itself, which
Shreve had designed and built in his Brownsville
machine shop during that busy winter. The Fulton
boats were all powered with low-pressure, vertical

steam engines with enormously heavy flywheel and condenser — an engine which for all its bulk produced relatively little power. Shreve's engine weighed a fraction as much, had no flywheel or condenser, and operated horizontal cylinders. It produced at least 100 horsepower (sensational for that time) and used far less fuel. Instead of being placed in the hold, it was mounted with the boilers on the main deck — a source of endless wonder to the fashionable passengers booked for its first voyage to New Orleans.

"Sure to blow up," said Shreve's dour detractors.

And in this second prediction Shreve's critics happened to be right.

Below Marietta, Ohio, a safety valve on one of the boilers stuck, the steam produced a dangerous pressure, and the boiler exploded, killing eight men immediately and scalding six others so badly they too soon died. Shreve himself had been thrown into the river and badly injured. He swam back to his stricken vessel and dragged himself along the deck to be of what aid he could to the injured and dying. He was but the first of many brave river captains who risked their lives to save passengers and crewmen in the hundreds of explosions which marred steamboat transportation in the years that lay ahead.

But even this disaster could not stop Henry Miller Shreve. He had the vessel repaired, and with a full complement of passengers and cargo continued down the river to New Orleans. He had promised his upriver neighbors that they would have steam transportation on the Ohio and the Mississippi, and that the port of New Orleans, freed from Spanish, French, and British threats, would not be blocked by the Fulton-Livingston interests.

Excitement ran high in New Orleans when it was learned that Captain Shreve, with a new and handsome steamboat, was blowing for a landing. In the gaily dressed assemblage on the levee was a tall and angry lawyer, Edward Livingston.

Captain Shreve welcomed him aboard with his usual courtesy, and Livingston, against his will, was greatly impressed with what he saw. Turning to Shreve he is reported to have said: "You deserve well of your country, young man; but we shall be compelled to beat you if we can."

Livingston was making no idle threat. To the consternation and fury of the New Orleanians, he repaid Shreve's courtesy by having the boat seized, and Shreve himself arrested.

Citizens of the port had not forgotten Shreve's bravery in the recent war; his rescue of hundreds of refugees fleeing the city; his running of the British blockade and manning of a gun during the Battle of New Orleans. Livingston, by contrast, had antagonized most of the town by seeking to grab an extensive piece of river frontage to which he had only the vaguest claim. Popular sentiment was in solid support of Captain Shreve.

This year, and the next, Attorney Duncan outwitted Livingston and his entire battery of lawyers. When Livingston seized the ship in 1816 and again in 1817, demanding $10,000 bail for its release, Duncan neatly turned the tables by insisting upon a $10,000 bond to be put up by Livingston to recompense Shreve for any financial losses caused by the delay. Livingston did not have the courage to go through with any such gamble. So he conceived another clever move. He offered Shreve one-half the monopoly if he would join the Fulton-Livingston interests. This was a very attractive bribe to a young river captain deeply in debt. But Shreve acted with predictable courage and honesty. He turned down this golden offer with "scorn and indignation," pointing out that the West looked to him for "free navigation of its waters."

Judge Dominick A. Hall of the United States District Court ruled against Livingston; and by 1819 Livingston himself renounced all claims to a monopoly of steam traffic on the lower Mississippi.

In 1824 Chief Justice Marshall of the United States Supreme Court handed down a decision, in the famous Gibbons *vs.* Ogden case which made forever free the use of all navigable waters within the United States. Captain Shreve had cleared one channel, and had made his historic contribution to American democracy.

But further struggles lay ahead.

In the next few years Shreve's various steamboats easily breasted the current, greatly shortening the time of the upriver run to Louisville. After the *Washington* had become too old for service he built the *George Washington*, the first three-decker on the river. His *Post Boy* carried the first mail by steamboat on waters west of the Alleghenies.

But all of these successes were not enough to satisfy this odd but admirable Quaker. He felt that he had cleared the channel of its legal blockade, now he must also clear it of the physical obstructions which menaced every steamboat on these rivers — the sunken forests of snags which every year took an appalling toll of boats and human lives.

In 1824 he drew the design for the strangest looking boat he had ever proposed to build. It was a steam-driven snag boat that looked like a great claw hammer, with the claw toward the prow, and steam hoists amidships. The object of the boat was to float this "claw" into an advantageous position on either side of a "planter" or "sawyer" so that the snag could be fastened to chains. Then the hoist could pull the great log completely out of the water.

Shreve offered his invention and his personal services to the Government, but it was another five years before they reluctantly appointed him Superintendent of Western River Improvement, and, with an inadequate allowance, financed the building of the first snag boat, the *Heliopolis*.

Shreve's courage was remarkable. For his first test he selected "the most dangerous place on the Mississippi River," a veritable graveyard of sunken ships called Plum Point. Within eleven hours he had removed an enormous tangle of snags, many of them six feet in diameter, and had made a clear, safe passage for even the largest steamers.

During the next nine months the *Heliopolis* and its sturdy crew worked steadily on the whole sweep of the Mississippi from the mouth of the Missouri to the Gulf, and by the last months of 1830 had cleared away forever the accumulation of snags which had been menacing the channel for hundreds of years. Trees would continue to tumble into the river, but their yearly removal was an easy job compared to that first Herculean task of uprooting the sunken forests left by centuries of former floods.

Seemingly the Government learns slowly. One would have thought that the War Department, observing Shreve's great success, would have been overjoyed to let him tackle the Great Raft which for more than 200 miles roofed-over the entire Red River of the South. Army engineers sent to investigate this tremendous log jam went back to Washington in dismay. They estimated that if the job could be done at all it would cost the Government more than three million dollars — an enormous sum in those early days.

Finally, with typical penuriousness, the Government granted Shreve a mere $21,663 to begin the work. With the courage and strength of a quiet Paul Bunyan, Shreve tackled the job, and in his first two days cleared five miles of the imbedded timbers. Behind his snag boat the river itself deepened its channel ten feet as the released water went rushing

toward the Mississippi. By 1838 the entire Great Raft had been removed at a total cost of $300,000, just ten per cent of the three million the Army engineers had predicted.

This opened hundreds of miles of navigable river, bringing steam transportation to vast reaches of fertile land in western Louisiana. Plantations and towns sprang up all along this route. It is little wonder that the grateful citizens named Shreveport for the quiet and dauntless man who had made their river a safe, deep waterway to the Mississippi.

Shreve eventually retired to a comfortable estate on the hills overlooking St. Louis. He had never become a wealthy man, but to the day of his death in 1851 he was beloved by his family, honored by rivermen and neighbors — a living legend who had "cleared the channel" of monopoly, and of forests of sunken trees. Like Nicholas Roosevelt, he was a true pioneer of the rivers — a man whose contribution to our national expansion can scarcely be overestimated.

8

The Pageant of the Packets

SHREVE's battle against the monopoly in the years following the War of 1812 sufficiently encouraged other steamboat builders so that in the years 1818 and 1819 sixty side-wheelers and stern-wheelers were launched on the Ohio and the Mississippi.

Apparently Shreve never attempted to patent most of his inventions or improvements, giving his knowledge and advice freely to fellow rivermen whom he seldom viewed as rivals. There was business enough for all in those early days of steamboating (although in later years competition between steamboat companies became not only keen but sometimes violent).

The first steamboat to reach St. Louis arrived in

1817 — a dingy little contraption named the *Zebulon M. Pike*. This caused a great stir among the citizens and in the local press. Two years later the arrival of any steamboat at this river port was taken more casually. But when in 1819 a steamboat made the first attempt to reach Franklin, two hundred miles up the Missouri, the excitement in St. Louis was again intense. Here was a promise of tapping the riches of the West without the slow and laborious process of poling and cordelling the heavily laden pirogues up the turbulent stream.

One of the most fascinating steamboats that ever struggled up the Missouri and the upper Mississippi was the *Western Engineer* designed and built at the United States Arsenal near Pittsburgh and launched in March 1819.

This curious, low-lying craft, painted shining black, had a carved wooden prow to resemble a dragon. The waste steam poured from the nostrils of the ferocious dragon-head, making a whistling, hissing sound which echoed from river bank to river bank and far into the forest.

The duties of this little steamboat were to carry army troops and military supplies to the soon-to-be-

established Fort Atkinson on the Missouri and if possible to Fort Snelling on the upper Mississippi.

But a secondary purpose was to "please and terrify" the Indians who were soon associating the Great White Father with this great black dragon. Whether or not this strange fire-canoe pleased the savages, it certainly terrified them, sending them screaming and howling into the hills. One Indian told his fellow tribesmen: "White man bad man, keep a great spirit chained to build fire under it to make it work a boat."*

* Quoted in *Steamboating on the Upper Mississippi* by William J. ("Steamboat Bill") Petersen, the best-informed historian on steamboat travel on waters above St. Louis.

Not only the *Western Engineer* but all of the early steamboats operating upstream from St. Louis were heavily involved in the transportation of military supplies and army personnel, as well as in the delivery of Indian goods. As yet the region was but thinly populated by whites, but a lively trade in pelts and in lead, mined at Galena and Dubuque, tempted captains of small steamboats to risk the many dangers of the upper Mississippi.

Both the Missouri and the northern reaches of the Mississippi were unnavigable from Thanksgiving to April because of ice. Actually, however, neither stream was particularly navigable even in the best of weather. The Missouri was choked with snags and shoals, and the upper Mississippi had two dangerous rapids, the Lower Rapids near the mouth of the Des Moines River and the Upper Rapids, even more swift and treacherous, a little above the mouth of the Rock River. Northward of these two obstructions the Mississippi was (and is) one of the most beautiful rivers in America with forested hills and bluffs on either side rising toward the sky, wooded islands, and exciting tributaries (some of them as large and navigable as the Wisconsin) pouring in from one bank or the other.

No obstruction, however, frightened those early steamboat captains, who in dire necessity sometimes ordered all the able-bodied men aboard into the stream to cordelle the vessel up the foaming, twisting, boulder-strewn channel. It was a race each spring to see which captain had the courage and skill to make the first upstream voyage of the year — an annual race to the head of navigation, near the thundering Falls of St. Anthony. To the victor belonged the spoils, meaning in this case the chance to purchase or transport some of the finest furs trapped by the Indians during the winter.

Today it seems almost incredible that steamboats were able to force their way up some of the smaller tributaries to villages now far from any navigable water. For instance, Abraham Lincoln's little stream, the Sangamon, across which a child may safely wade at almost any point, was penetrated in the spring of 1832 by a little steamboat named the *Talisman,* under the charter of Captain Vincent Bogue, who offered to deliver freight from St. Louis at a landing six miles north of Springfield, Illinois, "for thirty-seven-and-a-half cents per 100 pounds."

The village of New Salem, which was on this route, went wild with excitement, and twenty-three-year-old Abe Lincoln, already the veteran of two flatboat trips to New Orleans, led the volunteer labor gang which cleared away brush, snags, and other obstructions so that the vessel could work its way up this winding stream during the seasonal high water. Captain Bogue delivered his merchandise and took on a cargo of farm produce for the return voyage. But by this time the water was falling rapidly, and Lincoln was hired as co-pilot to assist in the difficult downstream journey.

The Fever River at Galena, Illinois, presents another mystery. Today it is hard to navigate it with a rowboat. And yet in the 1830's and 40's hundreds of steamboats somehow ascended this trickle of water to reach the harbor cupped between the mineral-rich hills some miles from the Mississippi. Galena, in fact, was the principal river port between St. Louis and St. Paul, and fortunes were made and lost by steamboat captains and owners, several of whom lived in this town and transported lead from the mines. It is thought that silt-laden water pumped from the mines deposited so much

sand and mud in the river that it slowly became a mere rivulet.

Oddest of all perhaps was the ambitious project to deepen a creek called the Salt River (which enters the Mississippi below Hannibal) into a navigable stream as far as its forks at the village of Florida, Missouri. This promise of river traffic was one of the attractions which brought John Marshall Clemens and his wife Jane to the town, and here a few months after their arrival in 1835 a frail little boy was born, a baby with red hair and green eyes who was promptly named Samuel Langhorne

Clemens, later known to the world as the beloved humorist, Mark Twain.*

Salt River was never deepened, and in a century and a quarter, Florida, Missouri, has not grown any larger than it was in 1835, but it made its contribution to river lore, nevertheless, by producing the

* A companion volume in this series entitled *Mark Twain and the River* will give the reader a much more detailed account of Mark Twain's entire career, with emphasis upon the importance of the Mississippi in his development. He was the great interpreter of the vast stream which courses through the best of his books — the magnificent, the mile-wide Mississippi, never to be forgotten by those who have read *The Adventures of Tom Sawyer, The Adventures of Huckleberry Finn,* and *Life on the Mississippi.*

incomparable writer who, as a carefree river boy, and later a skillful steamboat pilot, knew the Mississippi more intimately than any writer then or since.

Little Sammy and his family moved to Hannibal, Missouri, where he and his friends were soon climbing Holliday's Hill, "borrowing" rowboats to play pirate on the island, and exploring the cave. Sam and his barefooted pals always raced to the stone-paved wharf when they heard the welcome cry "S-t-e-a-mboat a-comin'." And here they gazed with endless fascination at the gaudy packets blowing for a landing — floating palaces to these one-gallus urchins, every one of whom had the "permanent ambition" to one day become a steamboat pilot. Sam Clemens and three of the Bowen boys lived to achieve that "universal" dream.

In an incredibly short time the Mississippi and its navigable tributaries had progressed from the flatboat to the steamboat era. It will be remembered that the first steamboat on the Ohio-Mississippi waterway began its adventuresome journey in 1811. By 1842, when Sam Clemens was seven years old, these inland rivers could boast more tonnage in steam than the entire British empire.

Mark Twain has not exaggerated the elaborate luxury of some of these vessels, particularly on the river below St. Louis. There were, for instance, three successive steamers named the *J. M. White*. A contemporary description of the third and most costly of these vessels will give some idea of the extravagant extremes to which rival boat builders would go to attract the highly profitable passenger traffic.

The third *J. M. White* had a melodious whistle with five tones, fancy stacks eighty-one feet tall, and a steering wheel so large that it took two men to turn it.

The main cabin was paneled in natural cherry, carved in filigree, and inlaid with other beautiful woods. This cabin could comfortably seat 250 passengers at meals, which for their variety and succulence were equal to any prepared by the greatest hotels. Twelve gilded candelabra hanging from the ceiling of this long cabin shone upon the gleaming, monogrammed silver and white napery, the gowns and jewels of the gamblers' women, and the diamonds in the stickpins of the more raffish gentlemen aboard.

There were seventy-three large staterooms, not including the two luxurious bridal suites and the comfortable cabins for the captain, the pilots and the other officers. All the staterooms were paneled in walnut and made comfortable with furniture of the same wood imported from France — each piece inlaid with lighter wood to fashion the boat's initials.

There were promenade decks and fore and aft galleries to accommodate 400 people. It was a very fast and graceful vessel which might have captured the antlers always awarded the swiftest steamboat plying between New Orleans and St. Louis. But Captain Tobin knew his engines were too powerful to "open her up" — and he made numerous records without racing, and without endangering his passengers. He had seen too many boats explode and burn to take chances with his valuable ship and the lives of those aboard.

Mark Twain, when he became a pilot, served at the wheel of many beautiful vessels and cut a striking figure in his white trousers, smart blue coat, and patent leather shoes. He was an expert on the multitude of chutes, crossings, and channels, reefs, bars, towheads, and islands in the 1200-mile run between New Orleans and St. Louis. He had learned the hard way under men as kindly but exacting as Horace Bixby, and as brutal and vicious as Tom Brown. He knew the "shape of the river" by day and by night, in flood and in low water, and could skirt or "climb over" the five hundred dangerous shoals and bars between St. Louis and New Orleans.

When Fort Sumter was fired upon, and the Civil War became inevitable, he helped pilot the last steamboat leaving New Orleans on the upriver run, and survived the "greeting" given the ship as she approached St. Louis where a cannon ball, fired by nervous gunners at Jefferson Barracks, smashed the glass of the pilot house, but fortunately missed the pilot.

The Civil War for a time disrupted the St. Louis–New Orleans traffic on the Mississippi. But each war America has fought, from the Black Hawk War against the Sac and Fox Indian tribes in 1832, through the Korean War and on to the present, has also created additional needs for floating transportation on our extensive inland river system. That is one of the reasons why Army engineers constantly guard and improve these vital waterways and maintain thousands of miles of 9-foot channel.

During the Black Hawk War, the Mexican War, and countless skirmishes with hostile Indians, river steamboats carried troops and supplies. During the Civil War, steamboats on the upper Mississippi moved midwestern boys to the battle zones, and brought back pitiful loads of the wounded, plus thousands of Southern prisoners. Entire books have been written on the struggle between Union and Confederate gunboats and shore batteries for mastery of the river, particularly around Vicksburg. After Union forces had again opened the Mississippi, steamboats and gunboats helped to hasten the northern victory.

After the surrender, far away in Virginia at Appomattox Court House, river traffic was resumed in a remarkably short time. The South was desperately poor, but somehow capital was found to build new steamboats in the South as well as in the North, some of them as famous as the *Natchez* and the *Robert E. Lee* whose memorable race won by the

Robert E. Lee has become a permanent and deeply ingrained part of American history and folklore. Millions of dollars changed hands between betting men on this classic contest, and it is safe to say that it will be remembered in song and story as long as the great river flows southward through mid-America.

After the Civil War some prophets of the new age of railroading began to see the handwriting on the wall and freely predicted doom for river steamboat traffic. Oddly enough, however, the railroads actually helped steamboating for the first two decades after Appomattox. This was due to the fact that most of the rail lines were being laid from east to west, while river traffic on the Mississippi ran from north to south. Often a railroad would be built to a terminus on the river and rest there for years before a bridge could be constructed to allow further extension westward. At these termini the steamboats took on the cargo, carrying it north or south, or west on the Missouri and other tributaries.

The prophets of doom were finally vindicated, however, when north-to-south railroad lines began to parallel the Mississippi. By the end of the 1880's the cry "S-t-e-a-mboat a-comin" was less frequently heard in river towns, and the beautiful and deep-toned steamboat whistles blew less often for a landing. A great and romantic era was coming to an end, but it continued to live in the minds and hearts of thousands of nostalgic people along the river — and particularly in the heart of Mark Twain.

Luckily Twain was able to make one last round trip on his beloved river in the spring of 1882 — taking the wheel himself part of the time between St. Louis and New Orleans. Through good fortune his old friend Horace Bixby was Captain of the boat, still upright and indestructible — the very spirit of the Mississippi.

From that last extended river voyage by America's great humorist, Mark Twain added to the material and rounded out the memories which helped him produce *Life on the Mississippi*. It also gave him the courage and inspiration to finish a manuscript he had long laid aside, his masterpiece, *The Adventures of Huckleberry Finn*.

9

The River Today and Tomorrow

IT IS a century and a half since Nicholas and Lydia
Roosevelt set forth through the wilderness on that
first steamboat voyage to New Orleans. Tens of
millions of Americans now populate the states bor-
dering the Ohio, the Mississippi, the Missouri, and
tributary streams. Great cities stand where the deer
came down to drink and the catamount screamed
in the "forests of the night."

But waters from fern-fringed fountainheads as
remote as the Alleghenies and the Rockies still
travel their ancient and tortuous pathways, to meet
at last and merge in the magnificent Mississippi,
rolling eternally toward the Gulf.

The Indian canoe, the flatboat, keelboat, and even

the great side-wheelers and stern-wheelers have left no lasting ripple upon the surface of these rivers.

While western civilization endures, however, this inland waterway will serve America faithfully as a source of inspiration to the imaginative, and a highway of commerce to the industrious.

The great days of steamboat travel are over. But the heavy freight moved each season far surpasses the tonnage of the packet-boat era. Huge diesel towboats, some of them costing between one and two million dollars, push (rather than pull) enormous tows of barges, linked together and laden with hundreds of freight-car loads of sand, coal, petroleum products, grain, chemicals, molasses, and various bulky objects too large for any railroad car, such as gigantic steel trusses and immense missiles.

One ton of freight transported one mile is called a "ton-mile." In a recent year these river barges rang up a total of more than fifty billion ton-miles, nearly five times the load they carried only twenty years previously. It has been estimated that the river system could transport all the freight now carried by railroads which parallel their course without the slightest traffic congestion. It is true that land transportation is faster, but it is also much more expensive. In peace, as in war (hot or cold) these great arteries of trade furnish the very life blood of industrial mid-America, and are almost as important to our survival and prosperity as our seagoing commerce.

Most of the towboats are kept immaculately clean, with comfortable living quarters for the officers and crew, lounges where the men off duty can read or play cards, and meals as wholesome and hearty as those served anywhere in the country. Even a short trip on one of these smooth-running, powerful towboats is a never-to-be-forgotten experience.

Owing to tradition however, ably assisted by the writings of Mark Twain, the old-fashioned steamboat will always seem more romantic than any towboat on the river.

As this is being written only one great overnight boat still plies the waters from Pittsburgh to New Orleans, and up the Mississippi to Minneapolis and St. Paul. This is the handsome stern-wheeler *Delta Queen,* whose home port is Cincinnati but whose itineraries span most of the 9-foot channel.

The *Delta Queen* is a piece of floating Americana that stirs emotions in every river town she passes and elicits greetings worthy of a queen whenever she docks or leaves a port. A wild cacophony of whistles from towboats, ferries, and other lesser craft join in the hail or farewell when she arrives or leaves New Orleans.

The history of the *Delta Queen* is romantic in itself. Originally fabricated in Glasgow, Scotland, she was shipped in parts and pieces to San Francisco where she operated as an overnight steamer to Sacramento on the river of that name. During World War II the Navy put her to work in San Francisco Bay, transporting troops to ocean-going ships.

At the end of the war, the Greene Line of Cincinnati (which in its heyday operated twenty-five river steamers) purchased the *Delta Queen,* encased much of the superstructure for ocean travel, towed her through the Panama Canal, and sent her up the Mississippi and Ohio to her present home port.

In January 1958, however, it looked as though this proud stern-wheeler had reached the end of

her career. Unprofitable despite the many passengers she carried to the Mardi Gras each year,
the vessel seemed headed for the scrap heap.

At this moment, however, there was a rescue as
dramatic as any to be found in a showboat melo-
drama. Two steamboat buffs, who were also music
lovers and calliope enthusiasts, joined forces to save
the *Queen*. Richard S. Simonton of Hollywood,
president of the Pacific Network of Los Angeles,
put through a long-distance call to his friend Edwin
J. Quinby, an electronics engineer of Summit, New
Jersey. They immediately agreed that the *Delta
Queen* must be purchased, refurbished, and saved
for a long and graceful life as the last of the overnight cruise ships.

"Since that bleak Washington's Birthday in 1958
when Dick Simonton, my son Jack and I gathered
at Cincinnati," Quinby says, "we have thoroughly
enjoyed every effort we have been able to make to
keep her alive. We arrived in the nick of time to
save the *Delta Queen* from an ignominious end.
This has not been easy nor inexpensive, but it has
been rewarding."

The big white boat, which is 285 feet long, with

a 58-foot beam, draws only seven feet of water —
somewhat less than the pioneer vessel Nick and
Lydia took downstream in 1811. It has an impressive 28-foot stern wheel which sends up a rainbow of mist when the sun shines through it, is
driven by powerful diesel engines and can comfortably accommodate more than two hundred passengers in its air-conditioned staterooms on the
cabin deck, Texas deck and sun deck. From the
engine room below to the pilot house atop the
vessel, it is kept polished and painted and scrubbed
and waxed like the museum piece it is.

The *Delta Queen* had only one flaw in the eyes of
the new owners. It had no calliope. And of what
use was a river boat — beautiful though she might
be — without a "steam piano"?

"Jay" Quinby as a very young man had played
the calliope for two wonderful weeks on the old
Ohio River showboat *Lulu Belle*. He was determined to find one of the few remaining instruments
to install on the *Delta Queen*. But of the sixty or
seventy calliopes ever manufactured in this country,
only three or four were still operating, and these
were all greatly treasured and unobtainable. Un-

willing to give up his search Quinby finally found a seventy-year-old calliope rescued from the showboat *Water Queen* which had been sunk by ice in the Kanawha River.

Eager as he was to buy, install, and play this 32-note steam organ, Quinby was not eager to endure the bath of live steam and glowing cinders, or the hot brass keys which were the "trial-by ordeal" which faced every calliopist of the past. Here his training as an electronics engineer came to his rescue. Preserving the thirty-two full-throated "whistles" which were still in tune, he introduced magnetic valves under the whistles and attached these to electric cables which led to a remote keyboard equipped with mercury contacts. Now the musician was not only protected from live steam and hot embers, but could achieve with the lightest touch chords and arpeggios which had taken the full strength of a strong man in the days of direct valve action.

Quinby made his own arrangements of such old-time favorites as "Sweet Genevieve," "Listen to the Mockingbird," and "Waiting for the Robert E. Lee." Sitting at the console of the *Delta Queen* calliope wearing his high silk hat and fancy vest, he looks like a riverboat gambler or a Kentucky Colonel. But the music he coaxes from those thirty-two keys brings crowds to the wharves of every river town where he puts on a concert. Colored spotlights tint the steam arising from the whistles, so his music can be seen as well as heard for at least five miles. When the *Delta Queen* docks at New Orleans for the Mardi Gras, you can hear the calliope as far away as Basin Street.

The *Delta Queen* makes round trips to New Orleans in the spring, stopping at several of the river towns, furnishing optional visits to the ante-bellum mansions, moving effortlessly along the Acadian Coast and operating as a floating hotel for its passengers during the gala events in New Orleans. For Civil War enthusiasts the trip up the Tennessee through the many great locks and lakes is a rare experience. At Pittsburgh Landing one may tour the now silent and peaceful countryside where the bloody battle of Shiloh took so many lives, and at Chattanooga one may visit Lookout Mountain where so many boys in blue and gray died — perhaps needlessly.

An autumn trip through the upper Mississippi Valley to St. Paul allows those of us who were brought up on Mark Twain to visit once again the town of Hannibal, and enjoy the rush of autumn colors which overtakes the forested bluffs as the boat moves serenely up the river to its ultimate goal below the Falls of St. Anthony.

While the *Delta Queen* is still afloat the old river days will remain a living memory. But even when she retires there will be traces of the past.

A few showboats, gambling boats, and daylight excursion boats remain to remind us of the time when mile-long rows of river steamers were tied up at New Orleans, St. Louis, and other river ports; when Negro roustabouts labored to stow aboard the heavy cotton bales, and in their leisure time made memorable music with their banjos and harmonizing voices. The hoop-skirted belles and river dandies have long since joined the more important phantoms of Lydia and Nick, the Quaker-garbed Shreve, and Mark Twain standing at the wheel.

But the river remains. The history of mankind is but a moment in the life span of this great stream which was here long before we arrived and will still be here long after we are gone.

INDEX